# UNCERTAIN FUTURE: COMMERCIAL BANKS and the THIRD WORLD

Richard E. Feinberg and
Valeriana Kallab, Editors

Contributors:
Lawrence J. Brainard
Karin Lissakers
Christine A. Bogdanowicz-Bindert
Paul M. Sacks
George J. Clark
Catherine Gwin
Benjamin J. Cohen

Transaction Books
New Brunswick (USA) and London (UK)

Copyright © 1984 by Overseas Development Council, Washington, D.C.

All rights reserved under International and Pan-American Copyright Conventions. No part of this book may be reproduced or transmitted in any form or by any means, electronic or mechanical, including photocopy, recording, or any information storage and retrieval system, without prior permission in writing from the publisher. All inquiries should be addressed to Transaction Books, Rutgers—The State University, New Brunswick, New Jersey 08903.

Library of Congress Catalog Number 84-8690
ISBN: 0-87855-989-2 (paper)
Printed in the United States of America

745

The opinions expressed in this volume are those of the authors and do not necessarily represent the views of the Overseas Development Council as an organization or of its individual officers or Board, Council, Program Advisory Committee, and staff members.

# Uncertain Future:
Commercial Banks
and the Third World

# Acknowledgments

*Series Editors and Project Directors:*
Richard E. Feinberg
Valeriana Kallab

*Associate Editor:*
Linda Starke

Many individuals have made valuable contributions to the preparation of this second volume in the Overseas Development Council's new series, U.S.-Third World Policy Perspectives. The editors especially wish to highlight the roles played by John W. Sewell, ODC president, and John P. Lewis, ODC senior advisor and chairman of the Program Advisory Committee, in the substantive planning of this volume, and to express thanks for the valuable comments and criticisms that they have provided along the way.

Members of the ODC Board and Program Advisory Committee called attention to various aspects of the Third World's debt crisis—and the role of commercial banks in helping to meet it—that merited analysis and policy advice in this volume; helped to identify some of the experts who subsequently agreed to contribute to this volume; and commented on manuscript drafts. Special thanks are due to ODC Board member Lawrence C. McQuade of W. R. Grace & Co. for enabling ODC to hold a small consultation in New York at which several experts—including Derek H. Hargreaves, Richard Herring, Roger M. Kubarych, and several members of the ODC Program Advisory Committee—contributed to the content planning of this volume. ODC Board member William H. Bolin and ODC Council member George J. Clark also contributed their views at the planning stages and provided valuable comments and criticisms in the course of the project.

The Council also wishes to express its appreciation to Stephen Low, director of the U.S. State Department's Foreign Service Institute, and to Leo J. Moser and Louis E. Kahn of the Institute's Center for the Study of Foreign Affairs, for co-sponsoring and organizing a conference focusing on the same theme as this volume. Most of the contributing authors presented early versions of their chapters at this conference and benefited from the exchange of views it enabled with invited executive branch officials, congressional staff members, and scholars.

The editors wish to express the Council's gratitude and their personal thanks to the authors for their close cooperation, dedication, grace, and good humor in meeting the demanding publication schedule set for this volume because of the timeliness and importance of the policy analysis it offers.

Special thanks for their respective roles in the editing and production of this volume go to Linda Starke, Carol Cramer, and Philip Murphy; and to Nellie Rimkus and Louise A. Fleischman for their valuable administrative assistance. Thanks for skillfully applying new techniques to the production of the manuscript go to Robin E. Ward and Marguerite Turner.

The Overseas Development Council gratefully acknowledges the help of the Ford, William and Flora Hewlett, and Rockefeller Foundations, whose financial support contributes to the preparation of this series.

# Contents

**Foreword,** by John W. Sewell ............................... ix

**Overview: Restoring Confidence in
International Credit Markets**
Richard E. Feinberg ........................................ 3

    The Importance of Banking .................................... 4
    From Boom to Bust in One Decade ............................. 6
    Rising Political Pressures ...................................... 9
    Grand Schemes for Debt Relief ................................ 11
    The Reform Agenda ......................................... 14

**Summaries of Recommendations** ........................... 21

1. **More Lending to the Third World?
A Banker's View**
Lawrence J. Brainard ....................................... 31

    Sovereign Lending and Market Disciplines ..................... 33
    Performance Criteria and Sovereign Reschedulings ............. 36
    Lessons of the Debt Crisis ................................... 39
    Changes in Bank Strategic Thinking .......................... 42
    Conclusions and Policy Implications .......................... 43

2. **Bank Regulation and International Debt**
Karin Lissakers ............................................. 45

    A Little History of Regulation ................................ 45
    Reforming the System ....................................... 50
    International Cooperation .................................... 61
    Conclusion ................................................. 66

3. **The Role of Information:
Closing the Barn Door?**
Christine A. Bogdanowicz-Bindert
and Paul M. Sacks .......................................... 69

    Setting Country Limits: Approaches of Major
      U.S. Banks in the 1970s .................................... 70
    Limiting Country Exposure: The Rescheduling Era
      of the 1980s .............................................. 73
    What More Can Be Done? .................................... 77

4. **Foreign Banks in the Domestic Markets of Developing Countries**
   George J. Clark ............................................. 79

   Reasons for International Bank Involvement .................... 80
   Advantages and Drawbacks to Host Nations ..................... 81
   Relationship Between Local Involvement
     and "Cross-Border" Banking ................................. 83
   Remittability of Domestic Earnings ............................ 83
   Policy Recommendations for Developing-Country
     Governments ................................................ 85
   Policy Recommendations for the U.S. Government ................ 85

5. **The IMF and the World Bank: Measures to Improve the System**
   Catherine Gwin ............................................. 87

   Evolution of the Relationship Between Official
     and Private Lenders ........................................ 87
   Sources of the Crisis ......................................... 90
   Reforms for the Future ....................................... 97

6. **High Finance, High Politics**
   Benjamin J. Cohen .......................................... 107

   New Policy Linkages: For Better or Worse? .................... 108
   Coping with Crisis in Latin America .......................... 111
   Can the IMF Serve U.S. Interests? ............................ 117
   Seeing the Debt Crisis For What It Is ........................ 122

---

About the Overseas Development Council
and the Contributors .......................................... 125

# Foreword

The past decade was marked by a major shift in the composition of financial transfers between the industrial countries and the developing world. In the 1960s, these transfers were dominated by Official Development Assistance—foreign aid—which accounted for as much as two-thirds of total financial transfers to the countries of the Third World. By 1982, foreign aid accounted for less than one-third of a much larger total. The roots of this shift are now well-known: the sudden surpluses of the oil-exporting countries and growing opportunities for productive investment in the developing countries.

The commercial banks of the industrial countries played a crucial role in the "recycling" of these surplus funds to the benefit of the economies of developed and developing countries alike. Now, however, the future of commercial-bank lending to developing countries is very uncertain—just when the stakes are greatest for the developing countries and the international financial system, as well as the banks themselves. For the Overseas Development Council, which seeks to analyze American interests in the economic and social progress of the developing countries, this raises two crucial issues: Will the commercial banks be able and willing to play a role in providing financing to developing countries in the future? And if they cannot (or will not), what new sources of funds can be put in place to support investment for development in these countries? These questions—which only a decade ago would not have been considered "development" issues—provide the impetus for this volume in ODC's new U.S.-Third World Policy Perspectives series.

Policy Perspectives, edited by Richard E. Feinberg and Valeriana Kallab, is a major new component of the Overseas Development Council's program. The series is designed to provide those who determine U.S. foreign policy and those who shape international development strategies—in both the public and private sectors—with policy-revelant, timely, and accessible analyses of important issues in U.S.-Third World relations.

Our focus in the series is on priority issues on which decisions are yet to be made; we seek to identify new policy options or new insights on the implications of proposals already being debated. In the selection of issues and the identification of analysts with expertise to address them, ODC benefits from the views of members of its Program Advisory Committee, listed at the end of this volume. All chapters are commissioned by the Council as part of its policy analysis program.

Like *Uncertain Future: The Commercial Banks and the Third World,* each book in the series will offer several perspectives on different aspects of a single policy theme. All of the analyses included will contain specific policy recommendations. While each volume will air differing opinions on the central theme, most of the contributing authors are likely to share ODC's basic persuasion that increased interdependence between the United States and developing countries is a *positive* historical development whose continuity requires vigorous, affirmative action by all parties, public and private.

Other institutions and their publications now analyze issues and provide recommendations for policy on various aspects of international economic relations or Third World economic and social development. But none do so with a specific focus on the *U.S.-Third World* dimension of international economic issues; this continues to be the unique trademark of ODC. We believe that a wealth of important and potentially useful research and analysis of immediate significance for policy making is generated in universities, research organizations, and private commercial institutions. Only a small fraction of this valuable work, however, is available to those who need it *when* they need it. ODC's programs, including the new policy series, strive to help fill this gap.

In initiating the Policy Perspectives series, the Council seeks to increase the frequency with which it calls attention to U.S.-Third World policy issues and highlights proposals for their resolution. The series will incorporate ODC's familiar *Agenda* series of U.S. policy assessments, *U.S. Foreign Policy and the Third World*, on a biennial basis; *Agenda 1985* will be issued in January. Subsequent volumes in the series scheduled for publication in 1985 include: *Trade Policy and Developing Countries* and *Development Strategies: A New Synthesis* (see detailed announcement at end of this volume).

We invite readers to send us their comments, criticisms, and suggestions on this and future volumes of Policy Perspectives, as well as their views on which issues need further clarification and might usefully be explored by ODC in future volumes of this series.

**August 1984**

John W. Sewell, *President*
*Overseas Development Council*

Uncertain Future:
Commercial Banks and the Third World

# Overview and Summaries of Recommendations

Overview

# Restoring Confidence in International Credit Markets

Richard E. Feinberg

A few years ago international banks enjoyed accolades throughout the industrial and developing world. The banks had become the main channel through which capital was transferred from North to South; they were providing a much bigger boost to economic development than the U.S. Agency for International Development or the World Bank. Today the private lending boom of the 1970s is blamed by many as the origin of the debt overhang that is choking economic growth in many developing countries and threatening the stability of the international financial system.

The debt crisis that burst onto the world stage in 1982 is a long-term problem, and we may not yet have witnessed its climax. Major outright defaults now seem improbable, but heightened conflict between creditors and debtors is possible unless bold actions are taken soon. The urgent task is to restore the creditworthiness of the major debtor nations and to strengthen the confidence of depositors and investors in the international capital markets. The objectives must be to minimize current losses to all parties, to create conditions that will permit debtors to maintain debt service while resuming growth, and to build international financial structures favorable to a gradual renewal of sound lending by the commercial banks.

New bank lending to many developing countries has slowed to a trickle. The immediate cause of the debt problem—the global recession and high real interest rates—reinforced the strategic planning decisions of many banks to emphasize new opportunities in domestic markets. In any event, a return to the rapid private credit expansion of the 1970s is neither desirable nor possible. But the combination of high interest rates and the retrenchment in bank lending is draining many Third World countries of badly needed development finance. New policies are needed that will reduce this unprecedented "financial flow gap" in private markets, while official lending agencies must fill some of the space vacated by the banks.

No single solution—no quick scheme of bail-outs or write-offs—can by itself resolve the crisis. Because capital markets are so complex and interlaced with other economic and political variables, a battery of reforms will be required. Most obviously, some industrial and developing countries should adopt more frugal fiscal policies that would, among other consequences, permit a lowering of international interest rates and improved credit ratings for some debtor nations. The resources of the multinational financial institutions—especially the International Monetary Fund and the World Bank—should be increased, and these institutions should learn to respond more assertively and flexibly to changing global financial conditions. The regulatory agencies that supervise international banking should work to improve the banks' balance sheets, particularly with regard to the adequacy of bank capital and reserve requirements against loan losses. And the commercial banks themselves must continue to improve their ability to gather, assess, and use information on country risk. Actions in each of these policy areas—macro-economic management, the programs of multilateral financial institutions, bank lending practices, and regulation—must aim at creating a more certain and stable environment for international capital flows. Some positive steps already have been taken, but much more remains to be done.

This volume focuses on the causes and nature of the apprehensions that currently grip international banking, the medium-term prospects for lending to developing nations, and the implications of these trends for Third World economies. It discusses the rapidly evolving roles of banks, governments, and international agencies as they try to cope with the swirl of events around them. It analyzes recent reforms undertaken by the U.S. government and others to contain the current crisis. Each author offers several specific policy proposals that are telescoped in the Summaries of Recommendations section that follows this thematic overview.[1]

## The Importance of Banking

Why should an entire volume in the ODC's U.S.-Third World Policy Perspectives series be devoted to a single industry and, more narrowly, to its international divisions? The answer lies in the strategic role of banking in the U.S. economy, as well as the banks' importance to the economies of developing countries. Banks channel savings from millions of small individual savers as well as from corporate and institutional treasuries to users of funds—corporate investors, individuals who consume on credit, and the government. Moreover, by lending to and borrowing from the federal government, banks fund deficit spending and also serve as a vehicle through which the government expands or contracts the money supply. In performing these activities, the banking system plays an important role in determining the levels of output and employment.

Precisely because of the pivotal position of banks, governments in the United States and elsewhere have intervened to assure their safety and soundness. As Karin Lissakers notes in an essay on regulation in this volume, banks in most countries are at once more closely supervised and more protected by government than are other commercial enterprises. Although the U.S. Congress has taken steps in recent years to deregulate banking, the industry remains subject to a high degree of government oversight.

The international operations of U.S. banks grew very rapidly during the 1970s. By 1983, the six largest banks had 54 per cent of their earning assets abroad.[2] On the downside, the exposure of nine large banks in only six major debtor nations averaged a potentially devastating 184 per cent of their shareholders' equity.[3] Furthermore, bank credit has traditionally provided the grease that lubricates international trade. The easy credit of the 1970s boosted U.S. exports, just as the recent contraction in international lending has cut into the foreign sales of U.S. producers.

Increasingly, the debt crisis is impinging on other areas of U.S. policy. The Federal Reserve Board worries that higher interest rates might push already hard-pressed debtors over the edge. The banks' international problems are causing Congress to reexamine the pace of deregulation for the entire financial industry. Those who make trade policy are acutely aware that their actions affect the ability of developing nations to earn the foreign exchange to service their debts.

International banking has also become a central issue in North-South relations. As a result of the boom in bank lending, the share of debt owed private financial institutions in the total outstanding medium- and long-term debt of the non-oil-exporting developing countries rose from under 25 per cent in the early 1970s to over 40 per cent by 1981. Banks became by far the most important external source of financing for imports and investment. Today the debt crisis has become a focus of tension between industrial and developing nations, especially in Latin America, where much of the debt is concentrated. The debt crisis has joined Central America at the top of the Western Hemisphere's diplomatic agenda. As Benjamin J. Cohen argues in this volume, the debt problem offers both opportunities and real dangers for U.S.-Latin American relations. The acute balance-of-payments squeeze—of which the debt crisis is a symptom—is contracting economies and disrupting social equilibria in many Latin American countries, undermining existing authoritarian regimes, menacing new democracies, and threatening to usher in a period of chronic social and political disorder. Many developing countries are also being forced to reexamine their development strategies—a subject explored in depth in *Adjustment Crisis in the Third World*, the first volume of the ODC's U.S.-Third World Policy Perspectives series.

## From Boom to Bust in One Decade

Given the severity of the current debt crisis, many people wonder why the banks lent so much in the first place. Yet it would be a mistake, as one banker wryly put it, to condemn the process as having been a history of "stupid loans by stupid bankers to stupid countries." Throughout the 1970s, powerful market forces, the internal structure of financial institutions, and the actions (or inactions) of governments made international lending seem rational and attractive.

The banks had strong motives for sharply increasing their lending to developing countries. The growth of the Eurocurrency markets—inflated by the large surpluses of the oil-exporting nations—injected liquid funds into the banking system at a time when demand in the industrial world was relatively weak due to slowed economic growth. (Also, the large corporations were increasingly able to bypass the banks and borrow directly from capital markets by issuing their own commercial paper.) The syndicating of Eurocurrency loans allowed the smaller, "regional" banks to take shares in loan packages. Fierce competition for market shares in apparently healthy and growing developing countries made banks more aggressive; loan officers were rewarded more for making loans than for denying applicants.

A market needs a seller and a buyer. The developing countries were eager to borrow to offset the higher costs of energy and other imports while maintaining strong growth rates. Given the low and sometimes even negative real interest rates of the 1970s, credit seemed cheap (although the banks protected themselves against rising rates by marketing their loans at floating or adjustable interest rates). Moreover, the banks were willing to extend loans rapidly, in large volumes, and generally with little interference in domestic economic policies.

Industrial-country governments and international institutions either encouraged this recycling or were largely passive. As Karin Lissakers comments in this study, national regulators were slow to impose discipline on the exploding Euromarkets and the practice of sovereign risk lending. In their separate essays, Lawrence Brainard and Catherine Gwin note that the IMF and the World Bank, despite some innovations, did not respond commensurately to the financial imbalances of the 1970s; and the loans authorized by the private banks soon far surpassed those of the Bretton Woods institutions.

The retrenchment in bank lending to developing countries happened even more suddenly than its expansion. Cyclical and secular factors converged in 1982 to deflate bank enthusiasm for most Third World markets.

Given that the IMF, the World Bank, and the U.S. Treasury failed to predict the length and depth of the global recession, the steep descent in commodity prices, or the sudden skyrocketing of real interest rates, commercial bankers can hardly be blamed for the cloudiness of their own crystal balls. Countries that seemed creditworthy in the dynamic 1970s were suddenly turned into dubious risks by events largely outside their control. The failure of many debtor governments to adjust promptly to the more adverse international environment of the early 1980s accelerated the transformation of good loans into bad ones; many governments continued to borrow in the vain hope that the global economy would quickly recover. As measured by the ratios of debt service to exports, reserves to imports, and so forth, the creditworthiness of many nations objectively slumped. Christine Bogdanowicz-Bindert and Paul Sacks observe that the banks' psychology—including their "herd instincts"—added to the gloom, to the point where defensive bankers reacted negatively to the very word "international." Those bank officers who supported continued lending to developing nations frequently met resistance from directors and stockholders who warned against "throwing good money after bad." The pessimists' case was strengthened by some members of Congress and national regulators who suddenly began to urge banks to increase their capital and reserves against potential losses.

Simultaneously, the same U.S. Congress and regulatory agencies were opening new horizons to commercial banks in domestic markets. As Lawrence Brainard explains in his contribution to this volume, many banks were eager to move into the increasingly deregulated fields of interstate banking and consumer lending, and into providing product services previously monopolized by investment bankers, brokerage houses, insurance agents, or real estate firms. Many smaller banks, which were especially anxious to curtail their international exposure, were staking out regional markets in the United States and concentrating on serving the more domestically oriented, medium-size corporations. The movement toward service-for-fee banking was reflected in the rise of bank profits derived from non-interest income, which for the major banks more than doubled between 1979 and 1983.[4]

Noting these trends in international and domestic markets, observers of the banking industry increasingly agree on the medium-term outlook for lending to non-oil-exporting developing countries. Lending is likely to increase at very modest levels, perhaps at about 5-7 per cent a year in nominal terms, which is near zero when inflation is taken into account. Even these modest increases may be difficult to sustain if the smaller, regional banks refuse to participate as they did in the 1970s. Some developing countries, especially in Latin America and Africa, may find themselves paying off more in principal than they receive in new loans as banks seek to discriminate more carefully among borrowers, concentrating on those countries in Asia and the Middle East that have lower debt-service ratios and on the traditional markets of Western Europe and Japan. Banks will remain cautious in international lending until they improve their own capital-loan ratios and until more developing countries are able to build healthier ratios of debt service to exports.

Banks will pursue their current strategies of minimizing losses and reducing perceived risk. They will retreat from large-scale, balance-of-payments syndications in favor of more traditional trade finance and loans tied more closely to collateral or project earnings, and they will attend to the needs of important corporate clients. At the same time, as George J. Clark explains in this volume, local currency markets—which do not involve foreign-exchange risk—may continue to provide fields for expansion where national regulations and the economic outlook are favorable.

Future lending levels will of course be influenced by many factors, including the direction of key economic variables and actions taken by governments and the international financial institutions. It is too early to predict whether more robust lending will recur in the 1990s. Bank decisions today and over the next decade will be heavily influenced by the management and resolution of the current debt crisis.

## Rising Political Pressures

So far, bank management has steered through the debt crisis with considerable skill. The sudden disturbances that have battered the financial system might have swamped a lesser industry. Despite the competitiveness and diversity among banks, the larger institutions succeeded in organizing and disciplining hundreds of their colleagues behind common solutions. In renegotiating some $100 billion of developing-country debt, the banks' leading negotiators shuttled from one capital to another to cope with many emergencies in quick succession. Bank officials worked hard and quickly in cooperation with the International Monetary Fund and the U.S. government to put together financial packages that kept major debtors afloat. Bank lawyers and accountants have worked creatively with federal regulators to find ways to avoid ruptures between creditors and debtors despite sometimes prolonged periods of partial non-payment. Rescheduling fees and wider interest-rate spreads on some Third World debts helped banks to weather 1982-83 while chalking up *rising* income. According to a Salomon Brothers survey, net interest revenue for the large, "money-center" banks rose from 2.38 per cent of total assets in 1981 to 2.85 per cent in 1983. Net income also rose, and dividends paid on common stock climbed from $1.7 billion to $2.1 billion.[5]

The immediate future, however, may prove more difficult. At the end of 1983, forty-two countries had accumulated external arrears totaling Special Drawing Rights (SDR) 26 billion, a fourfold increase since 1981.[6] Tightened federal regulations and interest payment delays from Argentina materially hurt bank earnings in the second quarter of 1984. Federal regulators placed five countries with relatively small debts to U.S. banks—Bolivia, Nicaragua, Poland, Sudan, and Zaire—on the "value impaired" list, thereby requiring banks to set aside reserves that are subtracted from profits. Bolivia unilaterally declared that it would limit its debt service to a percentage of its export revenues; this announcement did not necessarily mean that Bolivia would reduce its already deficient debt service, but it was a potentially disturbing precedent.

To date, the larger debtors have cautiously chosen to pursue independent strategies in their negotiations with the credit markets, while smaller debtors have seemed to lack leverage and organization. Nevertheless, many Latin American governments are under increasing political pressure to negotiate deals that force the banks "to share the burden of adjustment." A newly elected Argentinian government is facing public expectations of higher living standards. Many of its leaders were out of power or even exiled during the period of debt accumulation. In a publicly released letter dated June 9, 1984, Minister of the Economy Bernardo Grinspun unceremoniously told the IMF that the debt "was contracted through the application of an authoritarian, arbitrary economic policy in which the creditors actively participated, with no benefit whatsoever to the Argentine people—the great absent party in the entire process." Elections in Brazil in early 1985 could bring to power a government under similar stresses and with similar perceptions. At the same time, both the Venezuelan and Mexican governments are under growing pressure to end severe recessions in their countries. As Lance Taylor argued in his chapter on Mexico in *Adjustment Crisis in the Third World*, Mexico's President Miguel de la Madrid is likely to adopt more expansive economic policies as he moves into the second half of his six-year term. Thus domestic politics in the big four debtors may be converging toward tougher bargaining postures on debt.

In Chapter 6 of this volume, Benjamin J. Cohen describes these accumulating pressures. He finds that when the debt crisis first broke out, the U.S. government and the banks actually gained goodwill by quickly orchestrating rescue packages. More recently, however, Hemispheric relations are suffering from continued austerity in Latin America, high interest rates attributable at least in part to irresponsible U.S. fiscal policies, the perceived ideological rigidity and political heavy-handedness of the IMF,[7] continued retrenchment by private creditors, and the paucity of new initiatives to redress these serious problems. Many in the Third World believe that their governments have responsibly maintained debt service at great cost to domestic welfare, only to be slapped by rising international interest rates determined by policies set in New York and Washington.

The major debtors, and the Third World as a whole, are rapidly becoming net exporters of capital to the international credit markets. In 1983, Latin America owed about $22 billion in interest on commercial bank debt while receiving only some $7 billion in net new bank loans. Apart from "involuntary" loans that the IMF required to support its stabilization programs, the banks actually slightly contracted their Latin American exposure. The resulting "financial flow gap" of about $15 billion is not apparent from traditional balance-of-payments tables, which place interest payments among "services" paid in the current account but put credit flows in the capital account. However, juxtaposing interest payments and credit flows reflects more accurately the immediate impact of international capital markets on a country's external payments.

Latin Americans initially hoped that this historically and logically perverse outflow would be a momentary phenomenon. However, many leading bankers are now projecting a very modest growth in lending to developing countries of about 5 per cent a year, in line with 1983 trends. At that rate, if nominal interest rates remain high, the net outflow will gradually *increase*. There seems to be little prospect of a resumption of positive net flows in the 1980s, but unless the financial flow gap narrows, debtor governments are bound to become increasingly disgruntled.

These tensions are more likely to be diminished by bargains struck between creditors and debtors than by outright defaults. The developing nations will probably try to continue to increase diplomatic pressures to establish more favorable guidelines within which country-by-country debt packages can be hammered out. It is of course always possible that confrontational tactics by either creditors or debtors could lead to irrational or demagogic acts, but developing nations have several motives for avoiding a rupture with the banks. They recognize that default would risk access to existing trade credit and official finance (although countries now running trade surpluses are less vulnerable). The banks—themselves extremely interested in staving off disruptive and costly defaults—have continued to provide just enough new credits to make playing by the rules tolerable, while warning that default would jeopardize access to future credits. Countries making progress on their adjustment programs and maintaining debt service are being promised somewhat more favorable interest-rate and maturity terms for new and rescheduled loans. Added to these "sticks" and "carrots" is the threat that banks could petition the courts to tie up a wayward nation's trade and other international transactions. Moreover, most major debtor governments have their own reasons for not blatantly violating the sanctity of contracts: To do so might call into question the rules that govern their own social systems. Most local elites would not want to risk the unpredictable political consequences of repudiating—even at the international level—the moral and legal norms that operate at home.

## Grand Schemes for Debt Relief

Although most debtors have repeatedly voiced their intention to honor their financial obligations, they have been pressing for lower lending rates. These pleas have received some support from Federal Reserve Board Chairman Paul Volcker, who suggested banks explore placing a "cap" on interest payments (presumably as a means of gaining freedom for his monetary policies from the constraints imposed by the debt crisis). "Capitalization" involves postponing interest payments and rolling them into principal if market interest rates rise above a predetermined rate. An alternative would be to simply cancel payments above an interest-rate "cap." The capitalization approach would clearly be less disruptive for the banks, particularly if the regulators relaxed penalties for non-payment of interest. Postponement of interest has the same net effect as granting new loans and the same disadvantage: a weightier debt burden in the future. There is some support for "caps" among European and regional U.S. banks—who might prefer them to new loans—but considerable opposition from the heavily exposed U.S. banks. Lawrence Brainard warns in this volume that market confidence in bank profitability could be undermined by "caps," whose impact on bank earnings might be hard to predict given the volatility of market interest rates. However, Catherine Gwin and Benjamin J. Cohen consider the "cap" concept worth exploring.

An estimate of the impact of various interest-rate reductions on the earnings of U.S. banks suggests that there is some room for maneuver. Interest-rate concessions need not precipitate the collapse of the financial system. Under the more drastic "cap cancellation" approach, an interest-rate ceiling that reduced rates on existing loans by two percentage points for the four largest Latin American debtors (Argentina, Brazil, Mexico, and Venezuela) would only eliminate an estimated 13 per cent of earnings for the major U.S. banks, while a cut of five percentage points would reduce earnings by 33 per cent (see Table 1). While far from negligible, neither sacrifice would force banks to dip into their essential equity base. The impact would be softened by the fact that only about a half of these banks' assets are located abroad and by the tax relief that banks are allowed for losses. Nevertheless, sustaining such losses might well have an adverse effect on bank stocks and on bank capacity to sustain dividends. Whether the banks would also suffer a catastrophic loss of confidence would depend on the magnitude and likely duration of the concessions and the measures taken by the regulatory agencies.

The impact of interest capitalization could be further softened if it were linked to a formula requiring debtors to increase their debt-service payments in years of bountiful export performance. Furthermore, the IMF might expand its Compensatory Financing Facility (CFF)—which finances export shortfalls—to cover sudden increases in interest payments due to rising rates. This could allow the interest-rate "cap" to be set at a higher level. If the interest-rate-sensitive CFF were large enough, it might replace "cap" schemes altogether.

## Table 1. Impact of Two Illustrative "Caps" on the Interest Income[a] of Nine Money-Center Banks[b]

| Participating Debtor Countries | Reductions in Interest Income[a] If "cap" effects interest-rate reduction of: 2% : | If "cap" effects interest-rate reduction of: 5% : |
|---|---|---|
| Top Four Debtors[c] | 13% | 33% |
| All Latin American Countries | 16 | 41 |
| All Developing and Eastern European Countries[d] | 26 | 66 |

[a] After taxes.
[b] The nine money-center banks cited are Bank of America, Citibank, Chemical, Chase Manhattan, Morgan Guaranty Trust, Manufacturers Hanover, Continental Illinois, Bankers Trust, and First National Bank of Chicago. These nine banks hold 61 per cent of all U.S. bank exposure both to Latin America and to all developing countries and Eastern Europe.
[c] Argentina, Brazil, Mexico, Venezuela.
[d] Includes Yugoslavia but excludes the Soviet Union; excludes Middle Eastern capital-surplus oil exporters.

Method: Formula used for calculating hypothetical after-tax reductions in interest income: [(x%) (claims outstanding) (54 per cent marginal tax benefit)] divided by net 1983 income. This assumes maximum tax benefit; likely variation from this ideal tax position will increase the costs of charge-offs. It also assumes that the reduction due to capitalization is not listed on bank records as accrued income. If banks were permitted to record this money as yearly earnings, losses would be considerably less. All figures rounded to nearest whole number. Calculated by E. Scott Krigsman, Overseas Development Council.

Sources: Board of Governors of the Federal Reserve System, Comptroller of the Currency, Federal Deposit Insurance Corporation: "Country Exposure Information Reports"; and Bank Securities Department, Salomon Brothers, Inc., *A Review of Bank Performance: 1984 Edition* (New York: 1984).

Alternative proposals for resolving the debt crisis include the establishment of a debt agency, possibly connected to the IMF or the World Bank, that would purchase the banks' bad loans at a discount and then reschedule the loans at more favorable terms for the debtors. The Federal Deposit Insurance Corporation's purchase of bad loans—including some debts owed by private foreign firms—from the Continental Illinois Bank is a partial precedent. The Federal Reserve Board, however, could finance a large-scale buy-out of developing-country debt only at the risk of arousing a U.S.

Congress hostile to any perceived government "bail-out" of the banks. Unless Congressional attitudes shifted—perhaps in response to a looming panic in financial markets—the Fed would be jeopardizing its carefully guarded independence. An even less promising approach currently advocated by developing countries is to set debt service at some fixed percentage of export revenues. This idea is rather like homeowners tying their mortgage payments to their paychecks: an apparently "fair" deal but unfortunately unrelated to the cash-flow requirements of the bank.

Detractors argue that all of these plans—interest caps, asset-switching bail-outs, fixed debt-to-export ratios—are likely to impose losses on the banks, and at least indirectly on U.S. taxpayers, as well as to discourage new lending. Their supporters counter that the banks are hardly lending in any event. Moreover, they add, some losses are inevitable, and an orderly plan that dealt with the problem head-on might actually increase market confidence and boost the value of bank equities currently discounted for anticipated losses on Third World debt. Some bankers retort that such analyses are overly pessimistic or at least premature. Agreeing, decision makers have preferred to leave these schemes on the back burner as contingency plans for a more explosive or conflictive stage of the debt crisis. They prefer to wait, hoping that pressures will ease if interest rates decline or the balances of payments of developing countries improve.

To a great degree, the course of events will be beyond the control of the banks. For both the short and longer run, actions taken by others—the governments of the industrial and developing countries, official multilateral financial institutions, national regulators, and export credit agencies—will significantly determine the banks' fate. If these non-bank actors can successfully tackle a challenging agenda of incremental reforms, it should indeed be possible to shelve grand schemes for debt relief permanently.

## The Reform Agenda

The recession of the early 1980s caught the world with weakened international defenses. International capital markets had expanded tremendously, bringing great benefits, but also creating new and unforeseen problems that were unmasked by the global downturn. In proposing systemic reforms, contributors to this volume address several crucial issue areas: macro-economic policies, the policies of the Bretton Woods institutions, bank regulation, internal bank organization, and new financial instruments.

## Macro-Economic Discipline

The origins of the current crisis lie partly in disorderly macro-economic policies in many industrial and developing countries. Governments failed to pay adequate attention to the international implications of their fiscal and monetary policies. In particular, since 1981 the United States has pursued loose fiscal and relatively tight monetary policies that, among other things, contributed to high interest rates and an overvalued dollar. Many Third World governments have doggedly refused to accommodate their "domestic" budgets to constraints imposed by their integration into the international economy. Some have even seized upon the debt problem as an excuse for diverting attention from their own policy failures.

Lawrence Brainard's central conclusion is that a viable strategy to deal with the world debt crisis must begin by addressing the breakdown of disciplines in the fiscal policies of developed countries. Clearly, unless nominal interest rates fall below the rate of growth of developing-country exports, the key ratio of debt service to exports will continue to rise to the breaking point. Reducing the U.S. budget deficit will be a painful political task motivated by concern for the "domestic" economy, but the debate should also be cognizant of the budget's international ramifications—ramifications that feed back into the "domestic" economy. A decade ago, Richard Cooper noted that "trade policy is foreign policy."[8] Today, budget policy is also foreign policy.

For their part, many developing countries have already undertaken excruciating adjustments in expenditures that have slashed imports and current-account deficits. Nevertheless, many still suffer from very high rates of inflation, inefficient state enterprises, and widespread price distortions that hamper productive investment. As set out in *Adjustment Crisis in the Third World*, countries will have to hold down the growth of imports while they work hard to expand exports, thereby contributing to a gradual but steady decline in debt-export ratios and to an improved creditworthiness.

It is heartening to note the increasing recognition of the close linkage between finance and trade. If developing countries cannot export, they cannot earn the revenues to service their external debt. Thus the commercial banks have an additional motive to maintain their traditional support for an open trading system. Closer coordination is needed in the industrial countries among the agencies responsible for trade and finance. Concretely, official export credit and insurance agencies should seek to offset cyclical movements in external demand or in the availability of private trade credit.[9]

Although less frequently recognized, developing countries also have a responsibility to keep their own markets open to their neighbors' products, for South-South commerce has become important to the trade accounts of many Third World nations, including several of the major debtors.

**Strengthening the Multilateral Financial Institutions**

Public-sector institutions typically become more important during a period of economic turmoil. The relative loss of influence that the multilateral financial institutions suffered during the explosion of the private capital markets in the 1970s is now being reversed. Still to be defined are the appropriate roles for the International Monetary Fund and the World Bank once the immediate crisis is over.

It is in the interest of the commercial banks for the IMF and the World Bank to have the resources and authority to help assure a steadier flow of international credit. The Bretton Woods institutions will always face the difficult task of determining the most appropriate balance between finance and adjustment; but in the 1970s they were unable to impose enough adjustment, and in the 1980s they have failed to provide adequate finance. Catherine Gwin stresses that both official institutions have tended not to diminish but to reinforce global economic ups and downs. They should instead devise counter-cyclical policies to damp down fluctuations by increasing their lending during business troughs and by adopting more restrained measures during expansions.

The Bretton Woods institutions need more resources, but the budgetary constraints facing the major donors suggest that the official institutions also need to get a "bigger bang for their bucks." The catalytic potential of IMF and World Bank programs is especially important in periods of economic contraction and when private lenders and investors are skittish, as is the case today. Fortunately, both institutions recognize the logic of this argument. The IMF has boldly pressed the banks to increase their exposure in key debtor nations in support of stabilization programs. The World Bank has been working to increase its co-financing of projects with private lenders and is considering the establishment of a multilateral investment guarantee authority to stimulate the private flow of equity capital and, indirectly, of accompanying bank credits. Various other possible initiatives are suggested in this study.

In broader terms, several contributors to this volume conclude that the expansion of international capital markets and the increased financial interdependence among nations has not been accompanied by the establishment of new governing rules and institutions. There is no control over the creation of international liquidity. The breakdown of the fixed (or adjustable peg) exchange-rate regime has not led to more efficient or orderly adjustment. No formal mechanisms exist to coordinate nations' monetary policies, and lender-of-last-resort responsibilities remain largely with national monetary authorities. The logic of interdependence suggests that authority over global liquidity, exchange rates, and monetary policies should gradually shift from the national to the international level. If the IMF progressively assumes these functions and takes on the attributes of a world central bank, commercial banks would enjoy a more predictable and stable global economic environment.

### Improving Bank Regulation

National regulatory agencies must run the narrow course between overly strict regulations that stifle new lending and unduly lax oversight that allows imprudent lending. If they discourage any new lending, they will only exacerbate the crisis and further squeeze debtor liquidity. If they permit new loans that cannot be serviced, they will at best only postpone the problem and risk undermining the confidence of depositors and investors in the banks and the regulatory system itself.

Under pressure from the debt crisis and the U.S. Congress, the regulatory agencies have tightened the rules regarding capital adequacy, the establishment of reserves against loan losses, and the public release of information on the banks' international exposure. Karin Lissakers praises these first steps and argues that a relatively strict implementation of these regulations will place bank operations on a sounder footing. She finds that although U.S. banks have expanded their capital base by issuing more stock, European banks have more rapidly set aside reserves against potential losses and adjusted their accounts by marking down the value of dubious loans. Her view is supported by those bank stock analysts who argue that the banks will suffer further losses before the crisis abates.[10] In contrast, Benjamin J. Cohen highlights the desire of many debtor nations for an early revival of bank lending. However, reduced debt service—as a result of loan cancellations or interest-rate concessions—could have the same net flow effect for developing countries as new loans.

International banking is also governed by restrictions that developing countries place on foreign bank activities in local currency markets. Foreign banks operating within developing countries are often limited with regard to the number of branches and their share of the market and by requirements to have local partners. George J. Clark argues in favor of national treatment: Foreign banks should be subject to the same restrictions and have the same privileges as domestic banks, as is the case in large measure for branches of foreign banks operating in the United States. This would give U.S. banks greater access to markets that could be among the world's most dynamic in the future.

International banks might also benefit from the occasional imposition of stricter controls to impede capital flight from developing countries. Massive capital flight in Mexico, Venezuela, and Argentina, for example, has been a major factor in draining these nations of foreign exchange and generating their acute debt crises. Adjustment by more flexible exchange rates and more responsible fiscal and monetary policies is preferable and often inevitable; but as a second-best, interim measure, restrictions on capital flows and currency convertibility could be stabilizing. While capital can flee through many channels, clamping down on exchange and credit markets can at least temporarily slow the hemorrhaging.

Finally, both Gwin and Lissakers suggest that national regulators, perhaps in cooperation with the International Monetary Fund, should consider establishing target ranges for the future growth of international lending. The realization of this long-term objective would probably require that national monetary authorities cooperate more closely than is currently their practice.

### Internal Bank Organization

The debt crisis has had some salutary effects on banking operations. Management shake-ups, the questioning of old verities, and the reform of mechanisms for country-risk assessment are among the changes that should produce sounder banking practices.

Bankers and regulators have been cleansed of several illusions that were widely held during the heydays of the 1970s. Strictly speaking, "countries don't go bankrupt"; but it is now clear that they can have severe liquidity problems, may lack the political will to service their debt fully, and can even become insolvent if interest rates persistently exceed export growth. Banks also acted as though short-term exposure were relatively liquid and safe only to find that all banks cannot pull their credit lines at once. The sharp distinction between "commercial" and "sovereign" risks also proved to be overdrawn when otherwise healthy enterprises were ruined by large devaluations that inflated the value of their external debt in local currency, or when they were unable to obtain from a central bank the foreign exchange they needed to service their external debts.

Lawrence Brainard, Christine Bodganowicz-Bindert, and Paul Sacks all emphasize that the banks need to upgrade their ability to assess country creditworthiness. In the past, country-risk analysts not only suffered from inadequate economic and political data, but often lacked the status to affect decisions. Bogdanowicz-Bindert and Sacks find that many banks have both improved their ability to gather and analyze information and elevated the role of country-risk specialists and economists. They argue that these reforms be institutionalized so that they endure once the crisis atmosphere has dissipated.

Bogdanowicz-Bindert and Sacks also urge banks to do more to develop independent and, if possible, in-house capacities to accumulate and process information. The IMF and the World Bank also need to continue to refine their own systems for collecting and formatting data on external debt. In addition, Gwin suggests that the Fund and the Bank provide more technical assistance to help countries develop their own data bases. Deputy Secretary of the Treasury R.T. McNamar has suggested that it might be time to hold formal meetings to discuss information exchange among debtor and creditor governments, official institutions, and the commercial banks.[11]

**New Financial Instruments**

In the midst of the debt crisis, banks are retreating back to the familiarities of trade finance and project lending. Nevertheless, newer practices are also evident. Lawrence Brainard discusses his own bank's greater emphasis on making new loans with the goal of quickly selling them to other investors. Karin Lissakers would encourage the expansion of a secondary market for international loans, where banks can cash in old loans, if necessary at a discount. Other innovations are conceivable. For example, it has been suggested that banks might structure loans to private companies like convertible bonds—that is, they would convert to an equity position if rescheduling were required.[12] These schemes reflect the increased interest in flexibility, liquidity, and security—attributes that have taken on greater importance as a result of recent experience.

The reform agenda is challenging. Yet there is reason for some optimism about the possibility of action, since the key actors—governments in the North and South, the multilateral financial institutions, and the commercial banks—generally recognize that they share a common interest in developing less crisis-prone and more orderly international capital markets. This volume proposes a series of policies aimed both at engineering a deflation of the current crisis without a further deflation of the global economy, and at orchestrating a smooth transition to a future of healthy international lending.

## Notes

[1] Drafts of these articles, with one exception, were presented at a conference on May 22, 1984, jointly sponsored by the Overseas Development Council and the Center for the Study of Foreign Affairs of the State Department's Foreign Service Institute. The authors benefited from the discussion with the assembled Executive Branch officials and Congressional staff, and from the prepared comments of E. Paul Balabanis, Director of Planning and Economic Analysis, Bureau of Economic and Business Affairs, Department of State; Robert Dunn, Professor of Economics, George Washington University; James K. Galbraith, Deputy Director, Joint Economic Committee, U.S. Congress; Robert Gemmill, Staff Advisor, Federal Reserve; Richard J. Smith, Deputy Assistant Secretary for International Finance and Development, Bureau of Economic and Business Affairs, Department of State; and Alan Stoga, Senior Associate, Kissinger Associates.

[2] Goldman Sachs Research, "Investment Strategy Review: Multinational Banks," *Investment Research*, New York, May 31, 1984, p. 18.

[3] A. G. Becker Paribas Incorporated, "First Quarter Review and 1984 Outlook," Banking Industry, New York, May 9, 1984, p. 8.

[4] Bank Securities Department, Salomon Brothers, Inc., *A Review of Bank Performance: 1984 Edition* (New York: 1984), p. 17.

[5] Ibid., pp. 16, 25, 28.

[6] International Monetary Fund, *Annual Report on Exchange Arrangements and Exchange Restrictions* (Washington, D.C.: 1984).

[7] See Tony Killick et al., "The IMF: Case for a Change in Emphasis," in Richard E. Feinberg and Valeriana Kallab, eds., *Adjustment Crisis in the Third World* (New Brunswick, N.J.: Transaction Books, for the Overseas Development Council, 1984), pp. 59-81.

[8] Richard N. Cooper, "Trade Policy is Foreign Policy," *Foreign Policy*, No. 9 (Winter, 1972-73), pp. 18-36.

[9] For a discussion of the unfortunate tendency of export credit agencies to act procyclically, see Richard E. Feinberg, *Subsidizing Success: The Export-Import Bank in the U.S. Economy* (New York: Cambridge University Press, 1982), pp. 99-101. For a good case study of the recent contraction in trade credit, see William Bolin, "Central America: Economic Help is Workable Now," *Foreign Affairs*, Vol. 62, No. 5 (Summer 1984), pp. 1096-1106.

[10] See, for example, Goldman Sachs Research, "Investment Strategy Review: Multinational Banks," op. cit.; and A. G. Becker Paribas, "First Quarter Review and 1984 Outlook," op. cit.

[11] R. T. McNamar, "The International Debt Problem: Recent Progress and Future Ideas," remarks before the Davos Symposium, Davos, Switzerland, January 30, 1984.

[12] This idea is suggested in McNamar, "International Debt Problem," op. cit.

# Summaries of Recommendations

## 1. More Lending to the Third World?
## A Banker's View
## (Lawrence J. Brainard)

Bank attitudes toward sovereign lending are changing in ways that will fundamentally alter future flows of bank credit to developing countries. Uncertainties and instabilities in financial markets are causing banks to place increased priority on the protection of bank capital; more cautious and conservative lending policies are the result. Moreover, given current changes in bank business strategies, lending to sovereign borrowers will be less of a priority in the future than it was in the past.

    Several factors now act to deter the revival of bank confidence in sovereign lending. The breakdown of disciplines within the system of international payments has contributed to the growth and persistence of payments disequilibria and the accumulation of debt. Market variables such as interest rates have consequently been pushed to extreme levels in order to discipline policy behavior within the system. Banks are realizing that sovereign lending makes them dependent on others—primarily on the IMF—for the enforcement of economic performance criteria. The politicization of lending is further weakening the banks' ability to control their own credit decisions. Banks have also concluded that debt levels in borrowing countries were and still are excessive; and that increased official lending support—while desirable—will not by itself solve the problems facing the debtor countries. Finally, new proposals for imposing ceilings on interest rates and implementing multiyear reschedulings bring certain short-term advantages, but their longer-term shortcomings outweigh these attractions.

Public policies designed to assure adequate flows of external resources to developing countries need to be reassessed in light of these changing attitudes of banks toward sovereign lending. A viable strategy to deal with the debt crisis must address the factors that have contributed to the breakdown of disciplines in the fiscal and trade policies of developed countries. At the same time, the focus of debtor-country adjustment efforts should shift to the impediments created by heavy state intervention in the economy and by discrimination against foreign investment and private enterprise.

There are few signs today that changes in current policies in these areas will be forthcoming in the near future. This suggests that progress toward a solution of the debt crisis may be long in coming.

## 2. Bank Regulation and International Debt (Karin Lissakers)

The U.S. Congress recently enacted new legislation, the "International Lending Supervision Act of 1983," that for the first time establishes a comprehensive and uniform regulatory framework for the foreign operations of U.S. banks. Against the background of her analysis of the errors that led to the current crisis, the effect of the new legislation both on the banks and on the management of the international debt problem, and the current state of cooperation among bank regulatory authorities in the industrial countries, the author makes the following recommendations:

- The Congress should exercise its oversight function to ensure that the implementation of the 1983 Act fulfills Congress's intent. Requiring banks to face up to the consequences of their foreign lending by increasing capital, establishing adequate loan-loss reserves, writing down doubtful foreign loans, and fully reporting to stockholders the status of their international portfolios will strengthen the banking system and create the conditions necessary for solving the debt problem.

- International efforts to coordinate national bank supervision should go beyond the current focus on data consolidation, capital adequacy, lender-of-last-resort functions, and the allocation of supervisory responsibilities among national jurisdictions. Supervisory authorities should turn their attention to the instrumentalities of international lending—the large syndicated general balance-of-payments loans and loans with floating interest rates—and consider whether some other way of packaging international bank credit would be more conducive to sound banking. They should also consider the desirability and feasibility of putting some limits on the rate of growth of the Eurocurrency markets consistent with stable worldwide economic expansion.

- Monetary and regulatory authorities should encourage the growth of a secondary market for international bank loans that would allow banks to discount and sell off loans they no longer wish to hold.

- Disclosure requirements should be reviewed periodically. Perhaps the most effective safeguard against regulatory obsolescence would be to make disclosure requirements even more stringent, requiring banks to provide more information on their dealings with all foreign borrowers and not just where they have an unusually large concentration of loans. With more information, the private capital markets can play a greater role in disciplining banks and cover gaps that may emerge in the formal regulatory structure.

## 3. The Role of Information: Closing the Barn Door? (Christine A. Bogdanowicz-Bindert and Paul M. Sacks)

Perfect information about developing countries will never be available to banks, nor should this be as large a concern as policymakers have argued. If past experience is any indication of practice, information will be used to justify decisions already taken. For this reason, the authors are more concerned about the decision process within the banks—and the banks' ability to resist market forces and herd impulses—than about the current quality of country information.

The authors have the following suggestions for commercial banks:

- The information requirements of the 1980s are likely to be more stringent than is currently believed by some bankers, despite the decline in voluntary balance-of-payments lending to some parts of the world.

- Banks should resist reliance on other lending institutions for information and assessments related to sovereign lending, and seek ways to enhance the self confidence of the institution.
- Banks should build a country-risk system based on the more defensive lending environment of the 1980s and try to ensure maximum openness of the information system that feeds the exposure setting process.
- The energy devoted to econometric modeling could well be redirected into applying the insights of organization theory to international lending decisions.

The above improvements will not prevent banks from making some loans that are not justified on economic or financial grounds. However, banks have a reputation for short memories, and a defense mechanism should be built into the international lending decision process to assure that the next lending upswing is not the last.

## 4. Foreign Banks in the Domestic Markets of Developing Countries (George J. Clark)

The activities of international banks in domestic, local-currency markets have grown rapidly in recent years. The banks originally entered local markets to service their major corporate clients, but now concentrate on their local client base.

International banks may increase the efficiency of domestic markets by making them more competitive and efficient. However, the local banking community frequently perceives the large international banks as having unfair advantages in the domestic competition for business. As a result, many countries restrict the domestic activities of foreign banks in ways that discriminate against them in favor of domestic banks.

Long-standing official U.S. concern about such discriminatory practices has intensified since 1978, when Congress passed the International Banking Act, guaranteeing branches of foreign banks "national treatment," or the right to operate within the United States with the same privileges and under the same restrictions as domestic banks. At that time, Congress expressed concern about the competitive position of U.S. banks abroad; it asked the Treasury Department to study the matter and to report on it from time to time. Subsequent Treasury Department reviews of foreign government treatment of U.S. commercial banking organizations have found that many countries still maintain quite restrictive conditions on foreign banks—including outright and total exclusion.

Consequently, the author argues, it may now be necessary to introduce elements of reciprocity, as distinct from national treatment, into the regulatory process. Under reciprocity, U.S. operations of foreign banks would be restricted if the operations of U.S. banks in the foreign country were constrained beyond the restrictions imposed by the host country on its own commercial banks. A compromise might involve "reciprocal national treatment," whereby U.S. federal regulators would be charged by federal law to review the extent to which there is national treatment for U.S. commercial banks operating in specific foreign countries whenever foreign banks of those countries seek to avail themselves of national treatment in the U.S. market by applying for some new activity. Such additional discipline would require amendment of the International Banking Act of 1978.

## 5. The IMF and the World Bank: Measures to Improve the System (Catherine Gwin)

The debt-servicing crisis that erupted in the 1980s was not simply the result of too much borrowing and too much lending; the causes of the crisis were more complex and deeply rooted. The prolonged recession of the early 1980s caught the world with much weakened international defenses against global economic shocks and instabilities. The way that developing-country debt evolved over the course of the 1970s—becoming increasingly comprised of short-term loans at variable rates—left borrower nations particularly vulnerable to the economic pressures that erupted in the 1980s. And serious shortcomings in procedures for handling debt crises persisted into the 1980s, despite frequent past criticisms.

To help overcome these underlying sources of the crisis and lessen the likelihood of their repetition, the roles of the International Monetary Fund and the World Bank should be enhanced to: (a) improve each institution's capability to help countries absorb international shocks and cycles; (b) strengthen the Bank's and the Fund's catalytic roles in the promotion of additional, more stable, non-official financing; and (c) expand the activities of both institutions in ways that would help smooth the handling of debt crises.

In the case of the **International Monetary Fund**, the following reforms are recommended:
- Some way should be found—preferably through an enlargement of the Fund's Compensatory Financing Facility—to expand net lending substantially during periods of global recession.
- To foster more prudent growth of international credit in expansionary periods, an appropriate growth range for international lending should be regularly assessed by the key central banks in discussions held within the ambit of the Fund—involving the Fund's Managing Director in an advisory capacity, but leaving the central banks to use their own instruments to achieve agreed targets.
- Since the Fund's key role in helping to promote commercial lending is through its influence over the macro-economic policies of borrower countries, it should clarify that the purpose of its Extended Fund Facility (EFF) is to aid countries to adjust to a structural deficit and that this is an inherently lengthy process that tends to require substantial financing.
- The IMF might offer financing to smooth out *future* repayment streams instead of merely adding its financing to that of commercial banks at the time of a debt rescheduling.

In the case of the **World Bank**, key reforms might include:
- A substantial increase in non-project lending both to assist countries coping with economic shocks and cycles and to promote non-official financing.
- Use of the Bank's guarantee authority to help countries diversify their range of development financing instruments—including new non-bank financing and innovations in bank financing techniques.
- An active effort by the Bank to help a country mobilize public and private funds in the difficult recovery phase after a debt renegotiation is completed but before most private investors have regained confidence in the debtor's economy.

## 6. High Finance, High Politics
## (Benjamin J. Cohen)

The global debt crisis has become a central challenge to U.S. diplomacy in the Third World. In political terms, the key issue is whether debtor governments will be able to work their way through the crisis without being pushed by domestic pressures toward alienation from or confrontation with the United States.

More help will be needed from Washington at three levels—at all of which the debt crisis must be confronted as both an economic and a *political* problem:

- Additional financial and trade concessions are needed to keep political relationships from going sour. The United States must increase direct credit, guarantee, and insurance programs designed to sustain essential imports into debtor countries. It must also support increased funding for multilateral development institutions. Protectionist restrictions on debtor country exports must be avoided, and consideration should be given to the possibility of reducing existing restrictions on a non-reciprocal and, if need be, unilateral basis.
- A vigorous effort must be made to persuade the banks both to revive new lending and to be more forthcoming when existing debt is rescheduled. Banks should be encouraged to consolidate and reschedule debt on a multiyear basis, stretching out debt maturities as much as possible, and to reduce interest charges to the extent feasible. In particular, consideration should be given to an interest-rate cap that would permit "capitalization" of a portion of interest payments currently due.
- U.S. efforts must be maintained to ensure adequate resources for the IMF. The Fund's arrangements to borrow from member countries should be expanded to the extent possible. More important, the United States should take the lead in supporting borrowing by the Fund from the private markets, if necessary, to supplement its liquidity position. And in the absence of an interest-rate cap, speedy consideration should also be given to creation of a new interest-rate stabilization facility within the Fund to protect debtors against unexpected interest-rate increases.

# Uncertain Future: Commercial Banks and the Third World

Chapter 1

# More Lending to the Third World? A Banker's View

Lawrence J. Brainard

A vivid recollection from my early career in banking is a meeting that took place in early 1974, shortly after the first oil price shock. I joined a small group of senior bankers discussing the request of Denmark for a balance-of-payments credit. The key issue before us was whether private commercial banks had any business making unsecured loans to sovereign borrowers. After much soul searching, the request was turned down. Within a day, another bank had stepped in to underwrite the loan at a rate even lower than we had been considering. Within several months, the initial resistance of my banking colleagues to sovereign balance-of-payments lending gave way under the influence of competitive pressures. The large-scale expansion of bank lending to developing countries that followed is now history.

In view of the predicament they find themselves in today, many bankers are asking themselves a question not unlike the one that we struggled with in 1974: Can and should the private banking system be relied upon in the future to provide capital for sovereign borrowers in the developing world? If so, in what amounts and under what conditions? This is a pivotal issue facing the banks, the regulatory authorities, and those government officials responsible for international economic policy. Will a world economic recovery and austerity in developing countries reinstate market relations between bank lenders and country borrowers similar to those that existed prior to the present crisis? Currently most new bank lending to rescheduling countries is "involuntary" in the sense that principal refinancings and new loans are both necessary for the countries to make their current interest payments to banks. If a return to individual, uncoerced lending decisions ("voluntary lending") by banks is not likely in the next few years, then alternate policies must be considered.

Most studies addressing this issue so far have focused on projecting the balance-of-payments and debt positions of the major borrowing countries. In a study released in 1983, William Cline forecasted a relatively rapid economic recovery in key Latin American countries, which suggested that voluntary lending by banks might begin to be restored as early as 1985.[1] His assumptions of average LIBOR interest rates of 9 per cent in 1984 and 8 per cent in 1985-86 were, however, far too optimistic. An alternative scenario developed by Thomas Enders and Richard Mattione projected a substantial improvement in the Latin American economic situation by 1987, but the authors concluded that such gains probably would not be sufficient to restore "normal market relations" between the banks and borrowing countries.[2] The authors of both studies implicitly assumed that normal market relations mean resumption of a net positive flow of bank loans to developing countries.

Instead of concentrating on the prospects for world economic growth and developing-country adjustment, I approach the issue from the perspective of bank decision making. My central thesis is that bank attitudes toward sovereign lending are changing in ways that will fundamentally alter future flows of bank credit to developing countries. In discussing this approach here, my first objective is to assess the environment for sovereign lending in the period ahead. One dimension of this environment concerns the future stability of the international monetary system. A second concerns the integrity of the rescheduling process—that is, the extent to which the rescheduling process safeguards the capital banks have exposed in sovereign loans. Third is an assessment of several issues associated with current developments in the world debt crisis, my goal being to suggest how bankers interpret these trends and what types of conclusions they may draw from them. Last, I consider how the strategic thinking of the banks is evolving and how recent changes might affect their attitudes toward new sovereign lending.

The views expressed are my own. I make no claims that my assessment is representative of the larger universe of bankers; many of my colleagues undoubtedly will dispute parts or all of this analysis. By offering it, however, I hope to stimulate a discussion of the issues and consideration of their policy implications.

## Table 1. Share of Commercial-Bank Borrowing in the Current-Account Financing of Non-Oil Developing Countries (1974-83) (billions dollars)

|  | 1974-76[a] | 1977-79[a] | 1980 | 1981 | 1982 | 1983 |
|---|---|---|---|---|---|---|
| Current-Account Deficit | 38.6 | 44.9 | 87.7 | 109.1 | 82.2 | 56.4 |
| Net External Borrowing | 30.3 | 45.3 | 85.9 | 102.9 | 73.2 | 51.2 |
| Borrowing from Banks and Non-Bank Suppliers[b] | | | | | | |
| Long-Term | 14.7 | 21.7 | 38.4 | 50.9 | 22.3 | 43.1 |
| Short-Term | 7.7 | 7.5 | 22.2 | 19.6 | 14.0 | -22.9 |
| Total | 22.4 | 29.2 | 60.6 | 70.5 | 36.3 | 20.2 |
| Total Borrowing from Banks as Share of Net External Borrowing | 73.9% | 64.5% | 70.5% | 68.5% | 49.4% | 39.5% |

[a] Annual average.
[b] Bank borrowings account for most of these flows; a separate breakdown is unavailable.
Source: International Monetary Fund, Occasional Paper No. 27, *World Economic Outlook* (Washington, D.C.: April 1984), Table 31, p. 200.

## Sovereign Lending and Market Disciplines

The rapid expansion of bank lending to developing countries since 1974 is indicated in Table 1. After the first oil price shock, oil-importing countries had to adjust either by sharply restricting imports and domestic growth or by financing their balance-of-payments deficits through external borrowing. Most leaned in the direction of financing. Commercial banks played an indispensable role in providing the needed funds, thus easing the short-term adjustment burden of these countries. In so doing, the banks also helped the international system avoid a severe and prolonged economic depression.

The recycling of OPEC surpluses was strongly encouraged and supported by the governments of the key industrial countries. For political reasons, these governments were reluctant to attempt the mobilization of official capital that would have been required to recycle these moneys. Given the rigidities of official institutions, the option of private recycling provided a quick and flexible response to the dilemma faced by policy makers. In support of these recycling efforts, most major countries sought to stimulate economic recovery by means of strong monetary expansion during 1974-75 and thereafter. Initially this helped spur economic recovery. However, these policies also led to accelerating inflation, falling real interest rates (as market expectations lagged actual inflation trends), and rapid increases in borrowing (prompted by low and negative real rates of interest).

For the developing countries, the logic of the financing option in this new context still depended on achieving adjustment to the balance-of-payments disequilibria, now represented by the rising debt levels and continuing current-account deficits. Instead of taking place all at once, the adjustment needed to be spread over a period of several years. Unfortunately, in the post-1976 inflationary environment, it was easy to lose sight of the need for further adjustment. Developing-country exports were rising impressively; ratios of total debt service to exports were generally stable or were rising only moderately. This suggested that substantial adjustment had been achieved; the rapid growth of total debt and persistent payments deficits tended to be overlooked. The borrowers could also point to low or negative real interest rates in support of policies attempting to maximize their resource inflows and rates of domestic investment and growth. The oil-exporting countries, for their part, embarked on ambitious development programs based on their new earnings and expectations of more in the future.

The problem with all of this was that the foreign-exchange and capital markets lacked any real anchor. Rather than impose discipline on countries in payments disequilibrium, the system rewarded non-adjustment in the name of growth promotion. The failure of the industrial countries to pay attention to the new monetary order's lack of systemic foundations was, in my view, due to two factors. One was the huge magnitude of the oil shock itself, which led policy makers to put utmost priority on avoiding economic depression. The other was the shift to a floating foreign-exchange system in early 1973. The past disciplines of the Bretton Woods system were replaced by pragmatism and flexibility of exchange rates; the conventional wisdom of the day encouraged a complacency about payments disequilibria.

With the benefit of hindsight, it is clear that the system was operating under several serious misperceptions. The only effective constraint on sovereign borrowing was the willingness of the banks to grant new credits. In this inflationary environment, country adjustments appeared more substantial than they really were; country export successes reflected in large part the inflationary stimulus to prices and demand in the importing regions. As a result, the ability of countries to manage their debt burdens in a less inflationary environment was overestimated—not only by the banks, but also by the IMF and the World Bank. Judgments tended to become self-validating: New loans confirmed a country's creditworthiness and this perception generated even more loans. The IMF did not blow the whistle on country borrowing for a variety of reasons, and there were no regulatory limits or government warnings on bank lendings. Nobody wanted to argue with success and the judgment of the markets. The markets, in turn, took the silence of the authorities as tacit approval of their contribution to economic development in the Third World.

When Federal Reserve Board Chairman Paul Volcker threw out his anchor to turn the situation around in October 1979 by announcing strong anti-inflationary policies, the pressures for balance-of-payments adjustment mounted rapidly. Many borrowers and lenders were slow to recognize that the rules of the game had been changed; as a result, the strength and persistence of deflationary forces—particularly the effect of high real interest rates—was underestimated. This contributed to overoptimism about the growth prospects of the world economy in the period ahead. A full two years passed before the fundamental contradictions between trends in the real economy and the size of accumulated financial obligations were reflected in payments defaults by major borrowing countries.

Although the Federal Reserve's renewed policy emphasis on reducing inflation is welcome, the present system is far from satisfactory and in some respects worse than the one it replaced. The pattern of reacting to one disequilibrium (payments imbalances) by creating another (fiscal stimulation and inflation) continues.[3] Fiscal deficits in the United States and other industrial countries are substantially larger now than in the 1970s. The crucial difference is that the capital markets have learned to distrust governments' fiscal policies, while respecting the Federal Reserve's commitment to fighting inflation. The markets have responded by pushing prices to extreme levels—real interest rates are at all-time highs, and the dollar is substantially overvalued. The past decade has shown that if the only operative disciplines are those of the market, then market variables will be pushed to the limits of their plausible ranges. This is the price we pay for the lack of self-disciplines in today's international monetary system.

The lessons drawn from these experiences are that:

(1) Governments are unlikely to address the fundamental weaknesses of the world monetary system; economic disequilibria will tend to persist, contributing to instabilities in financial markets and to more frequent crises.
(2) Lacking the political will, governments will encourage others—banks, the IMF, the World Bank—to act.
(3) The de facto reliance on market disciplines in this environment increases the likelihood that greater variability and extreme values of market variables (i.e., interest rates, the value of the dollar) will be observed.

These factors place increasing stress on financial institutions. In the future, banks consequently will be placing top priority on the preservation and increase of bank capital. Cautious and conservative bank lending policies are to be expected.

## Performance Criteria and Sovereign Reschedulings

The willingness of the banks to resume new lending to sovereign borrowers now rescheduling debts will be influenced by the extent to which the banks' own interests are maintained and protected in the various rescheduling agreements. If the banks are happy with such provisions, they will resume new lending sooner than they would otherwise—assuming that other factors are unchanged.

In a typical corporate loan restructuring, an agreement defines creditor-debtor relations in three key areas: (1) the terms of payment restructuring and deferral (such as the interest rate or new maturity), (2) the status of various creditors (secured, non-secured, or subordinated), and (3) the ongoing controls imposed by the lenders on the company's management (the appointment of outside directors or managers, for example, or the prescription of financial targets and restrictions). In sovereign reschedulings, the first two concerns are prominent, but the third is not. Economic performance criteria are usually represented indirectly, by linking the agreement in various ways to the periodic disbursements of funds by the IMF under its existing programs. These disbursements, in turn, depend on the country's meeting quarterly Fund targets, or, failing this, receiving a waiver from the IMF for any shortfalls.

The major exception to the commercial banks' preference for piggybacking onto the IMF's performance criteria rather than imposing their own economic performance targets relates to conditions imposed on the treatment in the reschedulings of the foreign obligations of the private sector. In many of these agreements, the banks have negotiated clauses that require non-discriminatory access of private-sector debtors to foreign exchange at the central bank—thus enabling debtors to purchase foreign exchange with local currency for specified debt-servicing obligations (usually to make interest payments). Several of the agreements include the maintenance of preferential foreign-exchange rates for such purchases for a limited period of time.

Banks have been reluctant to negotiate economic performance criteria with sovereign borrowers for several reasons. Given the large number of creditors involved in each country rescheduling, banks have been particularly concerned to establish pro-rata treatment for all lenders and to restrict exemptions from such treatment. The large number of creditors makes it difficult to reach agreement on subjective management issues, let alone on differences due to political factors. U.S. banks might favor a hard-line policy in Poland, whereas German banks might not; in Mexico, the positions could be reversed. Many of the banks also still remember that a previous attempt to negotiate economic performance criteria ended in failure: The 1976 balance-of-payments loan to the Peruvian government showed that the banks had neither the ability to set out workable economic conditionality nor the willingness to implement the provisions of the loan, which called for various steps if the economic conditions were not met. Indeed, the IMF had to be brought in to salvage the situation after the banking refinancing failed.

As a practical matter, therefore, sovereign borrowers have retained leverage over the banks in matters relating to economic performance criteria. The banks' reliance on the IMF in this regard appears as a pragmatic and reasonable response to the situation that has existed until now. Banks typically have made fulfillment of IMF conditionality a precondition for the disbursements of new money in their agreements or for the principal rollovers of funds. The key performance criteria in bank rescheduling agreements boil down simply to the payment of interest and, in several cases, specified principal amounts.

The banks' lack of "control" (that is, their reliance on the IMF for economic performance disciplines in problem countries) must be seen as a fundamental weakness of bank lending to sovereign borrowers. This does not mean that banks are pulling out of such lending altogether. Rather, there is a return to old-fashioned rules of country creditworthiness, such as limiting lending to countries with low debt-service ratios—less than 20-25 per cent, for example, compared with ratios like Latin America's 40-60 per cent before the last recession. Banks are also concentrating on short-term, trade-related financing and, where possible, on project loans based on various forms of security (such as the pledging of assets or cash flow to the lenders).

Currently, banks are subject to strong political pressures to "reward" those countries that have successfully met their IMF program targets and interest obligations to the banks. Since the banks have faced annual negotiations with all of the countries rescheduling so far, the issue of rewarding performance under previous agreements has been addressed in an ad hoc fashion in the context of these new negotiations, through reduction of interest-rate spreads or lengthening maturities, for example. The main drawback to this approach is the difficulty of deciding where to draw the line without explicit common targets for all countries. After Mexico achieved a substantial reduction in rates in its 1984 new-money agreement with banks, other countries asked for these same rates—even though their actual performances varied widely. Banks felt pressed to grant some reductions in rates to all countries in subsequent negotiations. Indeed, some countries that are not rescheduling their debts now pay higher rates for new money than Mexico did in its 1984 agreement.

These developments have further politicized the banks' relations with the rescheduling countries. Countries that are unable or unwilling to "perform" also have brought—and will continue to bring—political pressures against the banks in an attempt to gain concessions. As bank-sovereign relations thus become highly politicized, performance criteria lose their meaning; this is what "losing control" means to a bank credit officer.

The overall situation regarding protection of the banks' interests via performance criteria is rather unsatisfactory and apt to remain that way for the time being. Determining who deserves to be rewarded would remain highly political even if explicit economic performance criteria were spelled out. Interest rates in various rescheduling agreements are not apt to reflect real differences in performance, however defined. As rising U.S. interest rates make it increasingly hard to reach payments targets, the debtor countries have sought political recourse in an effort to lessen the burden of adjustment they face. Rather than deal with the factors behind high interest rates, U.S. authorities have in turn recently sought to counter these pressures by shifting a greater part of the cost of higher rates onto the banks by encouraging interest-rate ceilings.

The results of these developments are not yet clear. Two strong negative factors for the banks do, however, stand out: One is that politicization of credit eliminates the banks' abilities to control their credit decisions. The other is that politicization weakens the role of economic performance criteria in lender-debtor relations, thus undermining the confidence necessary for a revival of sovereign lending.

## Lessons of the Debt Crisis

Beyond these broad, systemic concerns, several smaller issues also influence bank views about future lending to developing countries.

### Creditworthiness

An obvious lesson that banks draw from the past is that debt levels were and still are excessive for many countries. Before voluntary lending can revive in significant amounts, ways must be found to reduce country debt burdens. Under the best of external circumstances—continued world growth, lower U.S. interest rates, and rising commodity prices—it is unlikely that voluntary lending will begin in the next year or so. And even in this best case, many lenders would probably still wish to reduce their exposure levels. Thus a sustained current-account surplus and/or access to increased official financing would be a necessary precondition for the normalization of lender-borrower relations.

A second lesson relevant to the banks' assessments of creditworthiness is that more careful monitoring of country economic policy and performance is essential.[4] In retrospect, many banks failed to understand properly the political and economic dimensions of the policy environment that determined a country's debt-servicing capacity. A lack of relevant economic data often was to blame. The analyses also failed to consider assumptions that seemed unlikely at the time about interest rates, world growth, and commodity prices.

The challenge now facing the banks is to find ways to increase the likelihood that the various rescheduling agreements lead to the types of medium-term structural changes that increase a country's debt-servicing capacities. By entrusting the setting of economic performance criteria solely to the IMF, the banks leave a void. IMF involvement is an essential part of a longer-term adjustment process, but the Fund's programs, currently oriented to short-term criteria, will not automatically produce the structural reforms necessary for long-term recovery. A bank strategy to engage the World Bank and major industrial governments, in addition to the IMF, in developing *medium*-term structural adjustment efforts is needed for restoring country creditworthiness.

### Official Support

Increased levels of official lending to developing countries are needed. Additional debt—whether from public or private sources—of course increases a country's repayment burden. There is, however, a danger that needed structural changes cannot be achieved without greater liquidity. In the short term, more official lending can support a country's adjustment efforts by providing just that. In the longer term, increased productivity coupled with renewed external growth must help provide resources to service the debt.

Raising the level of official lending is also desirable from the banks' point of view in order to share the burden more equitably among various creditors. The banks fear that they may be putting up all the new money required or that the new money may be used to repay official lenders.

Some have suggested that major new programs of official lending on the order of a Marshall Plan for debtor countries is needed. But Europe after World War II possessed the ability to use capital productively; what it lacked was resources. Latin America's problems today are rather different. What is needed are access to developed-country markets, improved terms of trade, reductions in real interest rates, and more rational domestic economic policies. None of these is likely to result from a new large-scale lending program for debtors.

### New Initiatives

Several new initiatives have been proposed during 1984 in the context of discussions about future reschedulings. The most significant of these are "caps" (or ceilings) on interest rates and multiyear rescheduling (that is, rescheduling three or more years of future principal maturities).

Several general comments about new initiatives are in order. It is important, in my view, to preserve a case-by-case approach to individual reschedulings in order to differentiate between countries implementing, or not implementing, appropriate adjustment policies. Any "across-the-board" initiative rewards countries that do not deserve it.

Another concern relates to trade and working capital financing, primarily short-term interbank credits. If there is one clear priority among all the problems associated with the debt crisis, it is the need to keep trade flows moving. Trade and interbank commitments are vital to the continuation of exports and imports at levels necessary for economic survival, political stability, and future recovery. It is essential to preserve the banks' interest in maintaining these commitments on an ongoing basis. In most agreements, banks have exempted trade and interbank financing from rescheduling, although all banks generally have been asked to maintain the availability of financing in these categories at specified minimums.

The proposal for a cap on interest rates was highlighted in May 1984 in speeches by Federal Reserve Chairman Volcker and by outgoing Chairman of the Council of Economic Advisers Martin Feldstein.[5] The version they proposed implied a ceiling at today's interest rate; any rise in interest expense due to subsequent interest-rate increases would be added to the principal due (in other words, it would be capitalized). This approach reflected their concern that further interest-rate increases were probable during the rest of 1984 and into 1985.

An interest cap of this type clearly limits a country's payment burden and to varying degrees alleviates short-term cash-flow problems in a rising interest-rate environment. By so doing, such caps can improve a country's chances of meeting its short-term adjustment targets. This in turn may provide the encouragement necessary to continue with the adjustment effort.

On the negative side, interest-rate caps place the short-term risk of interest-rate increases on the banks. Over the longer term, they add to the country's overall debt burden by imposing interest on interest; in this sense, they are no more than a short-term palliative that lets the U.S. government off the hook. The accounting treatment of caps would also be unfavorable for banks, since the capitalized portion of interest (the excess over the cap) could not be included in income and probably would have to be shown as a nonperforming loan, at least barring a change in existing regulatory practices. It would be difficult for the markets to estimate the potential impact of such a cap on bank earnings, given the lack of knowledge about future interest-rate trends. This would add further uncertainty to already nervous financial markets. In light of the above comments about trade and interbank credits, interest-rate caps could not be applied to these without severe repercussions on future trade flows.

By comparison, multiyear reschedulings appear to be a less controversial issue. They eliminate the need for annual debt negotiations and handle the problem caused by the bunching of many maturities in the next few years. This could be beneficial, particularly to the debtor country. On the negative side, however, multiyear reschedulings could weaken the discipline of various performance criteria, since countries would not be obliged to return for annual negotiations. Since rescheduling seems probable for some time to come, multiyear rescheduling adds little except for economizing on the time spent in annual negotiations. Yet in return the banks must accept risks of a further loss of control and influence on economic policy management. On balance, therefore, such an approach could have the effect of moving away from the goal of restoring voluntary lending. It is doubtful that multiyear reschedulings will help rebuild confidence unless firm commitments to IMF and bank monitoring of economic policy management are part of the package.

## Changes in Bank Strategic Thinking

The recent recession brought to culmination a decade of rapid expansion in international lending; the problems of international debts have now moved to center-stage. At the same time, major changes have been taking place in the structure of the financial services industry in the United States. As a result, most institutions have been rethinking their business strategies for the years ahead. This reassessment also has been spurred by changes in the regulatory environment that increasingly emphasize capital adequacy.

Two types of changes predominate in new bank strategies. One is the increased focus on domestic activities, in part stimulated by the relaxation of past prohibitions on interstate banking. Many large banks with a strong commitment to consumer financial services are vigorously expanding geographically beyond their traditional home market. A second type of change concerns expansion into new product areas. A number of banks now emphasize investment or merchant banking, activities that have historically been left to the investment banking industry. At Bankers Trust Company, for example, a decision was taken seven years ago to de-emphasize retail banking and to add a new business focus—that of providing investment banking services to our customers in the United States and abroad. The process of shifting priorities during the intervening period has affected attitudes in the bank toward sovereign lending. A greater emphasis is now placed on the origination of new loans, with the goal of distributing (selling) these obligations to others, instead of making loans primarily to hold them in our portfolio. We no longer see the bank as a primary source of capital for borrowing countries but as an arranger or middleman of such financings. Given this focus, our new sovereign lending business has concentrated on top-quality borrowers in Europe and Asia.

The implication of these comments is that many banks are changing their business strategies; lending to sovereign countries will be less of a priority in the future. A number of banks, particularly regional ones, would like to reduce their sovereign exposure or get out of the business altogether. Thus, in a best-case scenario, the resumption of voluntary lending would require additional financial resources to repay banks choosing to reduce their exposure.

## Conclusions and Policy Implications

Bank attitudes toward sovereign lending are changing, in some respects perhaps irreversibly. Public policies designed to assure adequate flows of external resources to developing countries must take account of this fact.

My central conclusion is that a viable strategy to deal with the world debt crisis must begin by addressing the factors that have contributed to the breakdown of disciplines on developed countries' fiscal and trade policies. The path to sustainable world growth, lower interest rates, and rising levels of trade lies in the old-fashioned virtues of conservative fiscal management combined with reliance on free markets. Market disciplines coupled with fiscal irresponsibility will lead sooner or later to excessive strains on the financial system and a disruption in financial flows both domestically and internationally. In developing countries, such a situation could be lead to growing political instability.

The new initiatives that have been proposed—interest caps and multiyear rescheduling—have certain advantages in the short run, but these are outweighted by their shortcomings; if anything, they will discourage the desired revival of bank confidence. Increased official lending, on the other hand, is desirable for the many reasons cited. However, unless banks are able to understand just how governments intend to manage the debt crisis and unless they are offered realistic incentives to play a role in that process, more official lending will merely substitute for reduced private bank credits.

What role, then, should private banks play in the provision of capital for sovereign borrowers in the developing world? Although my discussion suggests a pessimistic conclusion, there have been a number of prominent success stories, primarily in Asia. These imply that a much more differentiated view of sovereign borrowers is needed, and the primary basis for making such a differentiation should be the efficiency and rationality of economic policy management in individual countries. It is not a coincidence, in my view, that many of the countries that got into trouble pursued policies of heavy state intervention in the economy and discrimination against foreign investment and private enterprise. It would seem overly optimistic to believe, however, that significant changes in such policies will be forthcoming anytime soon in Latin America. For that matter, prospects that the developed countries will start disciplining their economic policies seem equally remote. Thus progress toward a solution of the present crisis may be long in coming.

## Notes

[1] William R. Cline, *International Debt and the Stability of the World Economy* (Washington, D.C.: Institute for International Economics, 1983). For a critique of this analysis, see Albert Fishlow, "The Debt Crisis: Round Two Ahead?," in Richard E. Feinberg and Valeriana Kallab, eds., *Adjustment Crisis in the Third World* (New Brunswick, N.J.: Transaction Books, for the Overseas Development Council, 1984), pp. 31-58.

[2] Thomas O. Enders and Richard P. Mattione, *Latin America: The Crisis of Debt and Growth* (Washington, D.C.: The Brookings Institution, 1984).

[3] For a similar argument, see Colin I. Bradford, Jr., "The NICs: Confronting U.S. 'Autonomy'," in Feinberg and Kallab, *Adjustment Crisis*, op. cit., p. 119-38.

[4] This point is also underscored by the authors of Chapter 3 of this volume.

[5] "Volcker Terms Economy Strong Despite Rates," *Wall Street Journal*, May 14, 1984, p. 3; and Martin Feldstein, "International Debt Policy: The Next Steps," Remarks before the Council of the Americas, 15th Washington Conference, Washington, D.C. (May 8, 1984), p. 12.

# Chapter 2

# Bank Regulation and International Debt

## Karin Lissakers

The current international debt crisis has raised serious questions about the adequacy of bank regulation and supervision in the United States and the other industrial countries whose banks are the main creditors for Eastern Europe and Latin America. In the United States, the crisis has prompted Congress to enact a series of regulatory reforms pertaining to the foreign lending activities of American banks. These reforms in turn seem likely to force a change in the approach taken by banks, governments, and the International Monetary Fund in trying to contain and eventually solve the debt problem. The crisis has added an element of urgency to official efforts to harmonize national regulation with international banking.[1]

Before discussing these regulatory changes, it is useful to review the last decade of explosive growth in international lending and examine the role of regulation in that expansion.

## A Little History of Regulation

Banks hold a unique position in capitalist economies. They are major intermediaries between savers and investors, between producers and consumers. Most important, they are the principal instruments through which governments effectuate monetary policy. It is lending by banks that creates most of the money supply. The safety and soundness of banks—and public confidence that they are safe and sound—are central concerns of any government. As Federal Reserve Board Chairman Paul Volcker recently told Congress during a hearing on bank deregulation, "in normal circumstances and in most industries" a restructuring might be left to the free market, "but when the safety and soundness, broad confidence in banking institutions and continuity in the provision of money and payments services are at stake, competition alone cannot be relied upon to achieve the goals."[2]

In most countries, therefore, banks are both more closely supervised and more protected by government than are other commercial enterprises. Banking in the United States has been circumscribed by a myriad of restrictions—on where banks may locate, the range and pricing of their products, the services they may offer, the volume of business they may do with individual customers. And banks must open their books on demand for inspection by government examiners. Although Congress is taking steps to deregulate banking, and although many restrictions are being eased or eliminated, today the industry is still subject to a high degree of government intrusion.

At the same time, banks enjoy certain privileges. Competition has been limited by a ban on interstate banking and limits on the entry of non-banks into banking services. Banks are partially exempt from public disclosure of their operations. The government insures deposits up to a certain amount through the Federal Deposit Insurance Corporation (FDIC), giving banks a competitive edge in attracting funds.

Finally, the Federal Reserve stands ready to act as lender of last resort—to provide liquidity to banks in a crisis. Although a number of small banks have been allowed to fold during the recent recession, large commercial banks are protected against the ultimate discipline of the marketplace: the risk of failure. This policy was made explicit during the recent run on Continental Illinois, the nation's seventh largest bank. To try to keep the bank afloat, the FDIC announced it would fully guarantee all the Bank's deposits, whether insured or not, including Eurodollar deposits. Ultimately, in order to protect depositors, the FDIC took effective control of the bank.

### Exemption of Foreign Operations

The explosive growth of the Euromarkets and sovereign risk lending by banks in the 1970s, however, largely took place *outside* this regulatory framework. Although international operations account for 44 per cent of the earnings of the largest U.S. banks (Table 1),

**Table 1. International Earnings[a] of Ten Leading Banks (millions dollars and percentages of consolidated earnings)**

| | 1979 | | 1980 | | 1981 | | 1982 | | 1983 | |
|---|---|---|---|---|---|---|---|---|---|---|
| Citicorp | $355 | 65.3% | $323 | 63.7% | $346 | 62.3% | $508 | 68.0% | $468 | 54.8% |
| Chase Manhattan | 146 | 46.9 | 179 | 49.1 | 247 | 55.6 | 215 | 64.7 | 181 | 43.3 |
| BankAmerica Corp. | 225 | 37.4 | 287 | 44.4 | 282 | 63.1 | 247 | 62.7 | 185 | 49.7 |
| Manufacturers Hanover | 103 | 48.7 | 113 | 49.1 | 128 | 49.9 | 147 | 49.6 | 164 | 51.7 |
| J.P. Morgan & Co. | 150 | 52.2 | 216 | 59.3 | 259 | 68.0 | 283 | 64.0 | 250 | 54.2 |
| Chemical NY | 43 | 31.7 | 68 | 38.4 | 74 | 34.2 | 104 | 38.7 | 129 | 42.7 |
| Continental Illinois | 32 | 16.6 | 63 | 28.1 | 73 | 28.1 | 51 | 60.4 | 8 | 8.0 |
| Bankers Trust NY | 59 | 51.6 | 104 | 48.6 | 116 | 60.4 | 113 | 45.3 | 101 | 39.2 |
| First Chicago | 4 | 3.5 | −6 | −9.1 | 20 | 16.7 | 40 | 27.5 | 22 | 12.1 |
| Security Pacific | 18 | 10.9 | 24 | 12.9 | 53 | 25.4 | 74 | 31.6 | 46 | 17.4 |
| Total/Composite[b] | $1,136 | 42.4% | $1,370 | 46.0% | $1,598 | 51.9% | $1,782 | 55.8% | $1,554 | 44.0% |

[a] Net income basis.
[b] Weighted average.
Source: Adapted from Bank Securities Department, Salomon Brothers, Inc., *A Review of Bank Performance: 1984 Edition* (New York: 1984), Figure 41, p. 66.

this business has been subject to a minimum of regulation and, at best, spotty supervision—by either the U.S. government or those governments that host the Eurobanking subdivisions of American and other foreign banks. The reasons for this are historical, practical, and political.

National banking authorities are primarily concerned about and equipped to deal with the orderly management of domestic savings and credit flows, monetary growth, and the protection of domestic depositors, borrowers, and investors. Until recently, both the foreign operations of local banks and the non-domestic activities of foreign banks were viewed as largely irrelevant to these concerns. Thus U.S. regulators were slow to bring under close supervision the overseas transactions of U.S. banks in dollars or other currencies for use outside the country. And the authorities in Britain, West Germany, and other international banking centers typically control only those activities of foreign banks in their jurisdiction that involve the local currency and local non-bank borrowers and depositors. The rest, so-called Eurocurrency transactions, were treated with what former Federal Reserve Vice-Chairman James Robertson once called "competition in regulatory laxness."

The Eurocurrency market—the financial market for deposit taking and lending in currencies outside the jurisdiction of the issuing government—started out dealing primarily in dollars that had gone abroad as foreign investment or aid, or as payment for goods and services when the United States ran large trade deficits.[3] European governments were not particularly concerned when banks, either local or foreign, began to deal in these expatriate dollars. It seemed to have no impact on their own domestic banking and monetary concerns. Economists could never agree what the relationship was between the expatriate dollars and the U.S. money supply. The absence of reserve requirements, interest-rate ceilings, and other regulatory encumbrances made Eurocurrency banking highly profitable, and U.S. authorities could see no justification for denying U.S. banks the opportunity to compete. The market extended to sterling, German marks, yen, and other currencies.

London, Frankfurt, Zurich, and Luxembourg quickly grew into major international banking centers in the 1960s, and the host governments welcomed the jobs this created and the money brought into the local economies. The threat that banks would simply take their business elsewhere tended to squelch any suggestion that regulatory license should be replaced by closer official scrutiny. Offshore centers like the Bahamas and the Cayman Islands offered secrecy and non-interference and became virtual foreign bank fiefs.

Eurobanking did not seem to pose any special threat to the safety and soundness of domestic banking. In the 1960s, the banks' Euromarket clients were mostly the foreign subsidiaries of multinational corporations. Sovereign risk lending—lending to foreign countries—took off in the 1970s, greatly accelerating after the 1973 oil shock. The banks were then perceived to be saving the world economy. By recycling petrodollars, the banks enabled deficit countries to pay for oil and other imports and to maintain a higher level of economic activity than would otherwise have been possible. Bankers argued that any effort to regulate or closely supervise this activity would risk irritating the Arabs, who were supplying the petrodollar deposits, and would in general reduce the efficiency of the operation.[4] U.S. and European governments bought the argument.

Neither banks nor their governments showed much concern about the fact that, through the recycling process, the Western banks, rather than OPEC, were assuming the risk in financing deficit countries. The risk was thought to be minimal. Anthony Solomon, then Under Secretary of the Treasury (and now President of the Federal Reserve Bank of New York), could tell Congress in the fall of 1977: "In my view, there is absolutely no prospect of a debt rescheduling in regard to Mexico or Brazil. And I would not want to leave any impression that there is."[5]

Congressional pressure on the regulatory agencies to get a better handle on the foreign activities of U.S. banks did lead the Federal Reserve in late 1976 to review its supervisory approach to foreign lending. Certain changes were put into effect in 1978, including, for the first time, uniform examination standards among the three federal regulatory agencies for foreign lending supervision.[6]

But governments were slow to grasp the significance of developments in the mid-1970s. At the end of 1973, the Eurocurrency market was still only an estimated (no one kept precise track) $300 billion, including interbank transactions. Only a few large banks were involved. No one could foresee that in the next ten years the Euromarket would grow to $2 trillion, that national capital markets would become part of an integrated global market, and that banks would become integrated, global financial institutions. And no one anticipated that the process of integration and a boom in sovereign risk lending would eventually lead the entire international financial system to the edge of "the chasm down below," in the words of U.S. Treasury Secretary Donald Regan.

The debt crisis that began in 1982 with Mexico triggered the first national debate and comprehensive review since the 1920s of the regulatory framework that should govern the foreign activities of U.S. banks.

## Reforming the System

A Reagan administration request to Congress in 1983 for authorization of an $8.4 billion contribution to the International Monetary Fund became the vehicle for a protracted debate on government regulation of international banking. The discussions were shaped by differing theories about what had precipitated the debt crisis and what should be done about it. The administration and the banks argued that additional funding for the IMF was needed to help the growing number of countries in balance-of-payments trouble because of changes in the price of oil, soaring international interest rates, and worldwide recession. Many in Congress, however, charged that the IMF money would be used to "bail out" U.S. and other commercial banks that had loaned too much abroad and were now charging debtors too much for restructuring their finances.

Administration witnesses and bank representatives warned that tightening controls on bank lending to foreign countries at this time would discourage the banks from making more loans to cash-strapped troubled debtors, and thus put in jeopardy the rescue effort that had been launched to keep the debtor countries—and the banks—financially afloat.

In the end, Congress insisted on tighter rules for international operations of U.S. banks as the price of an IMF quota increase but left the regulatory agencies a good deal of flexibility in implementation. The "International Lending Supervision Act of 1983" states that:

> It is the policy of the Congress to assure that the economic health and stability of the United States and the other nations of the world shall not be adversely affected or threatened in the future by imprudent lending practices or inadequate supervision.
>
> This shall be achieved by strengthening the bank regulatory framework to encourage prudent private decisionmaking and by enhancing international coordination among bank regulatory authorities.

The Congress pressed reforms in three areas. It sought to give the private market a greater role in policing international banking by forcing banks to disclose more information about their foreign loans, to establish uniform regulatory standards that would discourage overlending in the future, and to beef up bank capital and loan-loss reserves to strengthen banks against potential losses on their existing foreign loans.

**Information on Foreign Lending**

Before 1983, the international operations sections of bank annual reports were masterpieces of obscurity. The institutions were not required to divulge to stockholders how much money they had loaned to individual countries (or borrowed from countries such as Saudi Arabia). Some banks listed regional exposures, but under categories like "Continental Europe," lumping loans to East and West, and "Western Hemisphere," grouping Canada with Central and Latin America. The reports never disclosed details such as the maturity distribution of country loans, or the proportion guaranteed by the U.S. government or multinational corporations with separate access to dollars. Banks were not required to identify troubled foreign loans or loan-loss reserves taken against them. The annual reports, in short, provided no basis on which an investor or a depositor could make even a crude judgment as to the soundness of a bank's foreign operations—thus inhibiting the market's ability to discipline banks engaging in unsound practices.

This presumably did not matter as long as bank regulators had enough information to do their job. In the early 1970s, however, regulators clearly did not. A handful of government examiners, with one office in London, were assigned to go out and look at the books of the hundreds of foreign branches (legally an integral part of the parent bank) and subsidiaries (separately incorporated) of U.S. banks. They were, moreover, barred from many countries. And there were no uniform standards for measuring country exposure. Each bank had its own system, and each regulatory agency had its own approach to the question. There was no comprehensive reporting by the banks on foreign lending that could give an accurate picture of the total international exposure of the U.S. banking system.

The situation gradually improved. In 1977, under pressure from Congress, federal regulatory agencies instituted the Country Exposure Report, requiring banks to report semi-annually on exposures subject to transfer risk, on a country-by-country basis; the banks' liabilities were also reported country by country.[7] Data based on these individual bank reports were made public by the Federal Financial Institutions Examination Council in a Country Risk Lending Survey.

The 1983 Act made the country risk reports quarterly instead of semi-annual and increased the amount of information made available to the public. Banks now have to publicly identify countries in which their exposure exceeds 1 per cent of total assets and to provide information on the size and status of such loans. Less detailed information is required for exposures over 0.75 per cent of assets, a provision that parallels a disclosure requirement enacted by the Securities and Exchange Commission earlier in 1983.

In implementing the 1983 Act, the regulatory agencies are asking banks for the first time to report the amounts of exposure that are covered by guarantees from the U.S. government and its agencies. The previous rule, whereby foreign loans guaranteed by the United States were treated as domestic exposure, had the unintended effect of understating total U.S. exposure in the country whose loans had been so guaranteed.

Public information is particularly important when formal supervision is lacking or weak. Congress should periodically review the new disclosure requirements to ensure that they keep pace with the changes that inevitably take place in the international banking market. Perhaps it makes sense for banks to disclose more detail on their dealings with all foreign countries. Information requirements are easier to change and to implement than regulatory reforms and may constitute the best safeguard against regulatory obsolescence.

## Loan Concentration

Congress also tackled the problem of the concentration of bank assets (loans) in a few nations. A small number of countries did the bulk of the borrowing from banks during the last ten years. Brazil, Mexico, and Argentina account for half the bank debt of developing countries. At the same time, a handful of large institutions did most of the sovereign risk lending by U.S. banks. The nine largest banks account for 60 per cent of the total $100 billion in U.S. bank claims on non-OPEC developing countries, while the 24 largest banks hold 80 per cent of such claims.[8] It follows that there is a high degree of country-risk concentration in the portfolios of the big banks: The loan exposure of the nine largest banks to the twelve largest developing-country borrowers equals 210 per cent of their aggregate capital (see Table 2).

By concentrating their lending in a few countries, the banks violated a cardinal rule of prudent banking: that portfolios should be diversified and risks spread among many different customers. Indeed, U.S. banks are subject to a legal lending limit of 15 per cent of capital to any one borrower (raised from 10 per cent in 1983), so

**Table 2. Exposure of Nine Money-Center Banks[a] to Twelve Largest Developing-Country Borrowers (millions dollars)**

|  | 30 June 83 | 31 Dec. 82 | 30 June 82 | Total Capital[b] | Exposure of all U.S. Banks |
|---|---|---|---|---|---|
| | | | | Banks' Exposure as of 30 June 83 as a Percentage of | |
| Mexico | $13,422 | $12,862 | $13,443 | 44.4% | 54.9% |
| Brazil | 13,280 | 13,296 | 11,775 | 44.0 | 64.7 |
| Venezuela | 7,575 | 7,804 | 7,313 | 25.1 | 67.9 |
| South Korea | 6,307 | 7,134 | 5,120 | 20.9 | 59.4 |
| Argentina | 5,215 | 5,125 | 5,331 | 17.3 | 62.1 |
| Philippines | 3,942 | 3,882 | 3,907 | 13.1 | 67.1 |
| Chile | 3,065 | 3,327 | 3,364 | 10.2 | 54.6 |
| Taiwan | 2,808 | 3,047 | 2,698 | 9.3 | 66.2 |
| Indonesia | 2,723 | 2,501 | 2,147 | 9.0 | 84.3 |
| Colombia | 2,263 | 2,225 | 1,859 | 7.5 | 67.9 |
| Peru | 1,463 | 1,364 | 1,354 | 4.8 | 55.7 |
| Yugoslavia | 1,460 | 1,461 | 1,497 | 4.8 | 62.5 |
| TOTAL | $63,523 | $64,028 | $59,808 | 210.4% | 62.0% |

[a] The nine money-center banks cited are Bank of America, Citibank, Chemical, Chase Manhattan, Morgan Guaranty Trust, Manufacturers Hanover, Continental Illinois, Bankers Trust, and First National Bank of Chicago.

[b] Total capital of the nine money-center banks includes equity, subordinated debentures and provisions for loan losses; as of June 30, 1983, it totaled $30.2 billion.

Source: Adapted from Bank Securities Department, Salomon Brothers, Inc., *A Review of Bank Performance: 1984 Edition* (New York: 1984), Figure 45, p. 70.

that the default of one borrower or even a number of borrowers should not endanger the bank.

The legal lending limit covers foreign as well as domestic borrowers. But as applied to sovereign risk lending during the 1970s, the rule was for all practical purposes meaningless. State agencies and enterprises of one kind or another account for much of the foreign borrowing done by Eastern Europe and the Third World. Yet these borrowers were treated by the banks and the regulators for purposes of the lending limit as if they were separate and distinct borrowers.

In 1978, the Comptroller of the Currency sought to correct this by applying a "means and uses" test. Loans to foreign state agencies with an independent source of revenue (such as a state oil company, borrowing on its own behalf) would be treated as a single borrower; loans to state agencies dependent on the government treasury and borrowing for general government-financing purposes would be lumped with other loans to the central government for legal lending-limit purposes.

But this reform did not solve the problem of transfer risk. That is, most sovereign loans are denominated in hard currencies—U.S. dollars, German marks, Swiss francs, yen. Ninety-five per cent of Latin America's bank debts are denominated in dollars. Borrowers in these countries, whether private corporations or state enterprises, generally depend on the central bank to make available the foreign exchange needed to service their loans. When the central bank is short of foreign exchange, every debtor without an external source of dollars, marks, or other needed currency will have trouble servicing its foreign debt.

Efforts to limit country-risk concentration by supervisory means were not much more successful. Before 1977, it was up to individual bank examiners to classify countries and loans as high risk. There was no specific measure of loan concentration by country. Categories traditionally used by examiners to classify above-normal commercial credit risk—"special mention," "substandard," "doubtful," and "loss"—were sometimes applied to countries. This process, which was supposed to be confidential, created an awkward diplomatic situation when word leaked out that regulators had classified loans to Italy as subject to "special mention."

After 1977, an Inter-Agency Country Exposure Review Committee composed of examiners from the federal regulatory agencies decided which countries should be classified as above-normal risk. It also began to rate countries as "strong," "moderately strong," or "weak." As part of the new examination process, examiners looked at the adequacy of individual banks' country-risk evaluation systems. Advisory prudential lending limits relative to capital were then set according to a country's rating, and examiners would bring excessive country exposures to the attention of bank management. But as Federal Reserve Governor Henry Wallich has pointed out, "while examiner comments have made management and boards of directors more conscious of country concentrations, the system has had no further explicit supervisory penalty. Therefore, it has not necessarily affected bank lending policy."[9] In other words, banks often ignored government examiners. Indeed, the concentration of U.S. bank loans to Latin America increased significantly after the new review procedures were in place.

In the course of the U.S. congressional debate on the IMF funding increase, bank regulators successfully fought off demands for some form of country-by-country lending limits. With the backing of the Treasury and State Departments, they argued that country-specific limits would be politically sensitive to the countries in question.

More importantly, a flat country limit would present practical problems, given that the exposure of some banks to the biggest Latin American borrowers already far exceeds what could be considered a prudent level. Several New York banks have loaned the equivalent of more than 70 per cent of capital to Brazil and more than 50 per cent of capital to Mexico. (The recommended lending limit for "strong" countries was 25 per cent.) Setting the limit above that would be meaningless and setting the limit below would effectively bar those banks from making more loans to the most seriously troubled debtors. And that would in turn sabotage the strategy devised by the Federal Reserve, the banks, and the IMF to deal with the immediate debt crisis—to keep all creditors lending enough new money to enable the debtors to stay current on interest payments while "adjusting" their economies to the new reality of a much reduced credit flow.

Congress and the regulators got at the problem of loan concentration indirectly, through capital adequacy.

### Capital Adequacy

In recent years, banking authorities have become increasingly concerned about the steady drop in the ratio of capital (shareholders' equity plus reserves and subordinated long-term debt) to assets. Banks, after all, lend other people's money—depositors' money and borrowed funds—not their own. When a loan goes bad, a bank has to dip into its current and retained earnings and, if necessary, equity (its own money) to honor its deposits. When losses exceed earnings and capital, a bank is bust. Bank capital also gives the stockholders a direct stake in honest management of the bank.

Although capital adequacy has always been an important benchmark for bank examiners, there was until recently no firm federal minimum capital requirement for the large multinational banks, the banks most heavily involved in international banking. It was precisely those banks' ratios that had shown the most dramatic decline. When their capital-to-assets ratios began to drop below 4 per cent (and even lower, if one counts only equity), the regulatory agencies finally acted; in the summer of 1983, they set a minimum of 5 per cent of assets for large banks.

But the foreign loans, as already noted, pose a special problem. As of the end of 1982, Manufacturers Hanover's exposure to the three biggest troubled Latin borrowers was equal to 190 per cent of capital, Citibank's exposure to the same three countries was 145 per cent of capital, and Chase Manhattan's was 118 per cent. The exposure of all U.S. banks to Eastern Europe, non-oil developing countries, and non-capital-surplus OPEC countries was nearly 200 per cent of capital.[10] There is reason to question whether a ratio of 5 per cent capital to assets is really an adequate cushion when a bank's assets include so many shaky loans.

The 1983 Act therefore authorizes the regulators to require banks with large concentrations of lending to a particular country to maintain a higher ratio of capital to total assets than is required of banks with more diversified portfolios. A ratio of 7 to 10 per cent of capital might be necessary to provide an adequate cushion against existing exposures and a strong deterrent against future excesses. Historically, 10 per cent was the "correct" ratio for nationally chartered U.S. banks. But there is no evidence that regulators are prepared to push the banks that hard.

### Treatment of Troubled Loans

Two thirds of U.S. bank loans to Eastern Europe, non-oil developing countries, and non-capital-surplus oil exporters have been subject to payments disruption since 1982.[11] The first sign that a loan is in trouble is usually a missed payment of principal or interest by the borrower. The former is less problematic for a bank from a bookkeeping standpoint (and in banking, it often comes down to bookkeeping): A new schedule of repayment can be negotiated, usually at a higher interest, if necessary with a grace period in which no payments of principal need be made. This is the approach commonly taken with foreign-country debtors. Billions of dollars in payments due from Eastern Europe and from Latin America have been rescheduled in the last two years, with grace periods of up to three to five years. Much of Latin America is making no principal repayments on medium-term debt at all at this time.

Treatment of interest payments is trickier. Banks, of course, have to continue funding outstanding loans. Interest payments are needed to cover the cost of these funds—that is, to pay interest to depositors or other banks from which the funds were "bought"—and to yield the bank a profit. Banks are allowed to report interest earnings as if they had been received in the quarter in which they were due, even though actual payment may be late. But once interest payments are more than 90 days in arrears, state and federal regulations require that a loan be put on "non-accrual," and missed interest payments may have to be deducted from previously reported earnings. A lot of non-accruing loans can quickly wipe out a bank's profits.

Until June 1984, regulators had actually allowed banks to keep loans on accrual beyond the 90-day deadline, provided that the arrearages were made up before the end of each quarter. Thus Argentine loans, for example, could be carried as accruing in February, although they were four months in arrears—provided that Argentina reduced the arrearages to less than 90 days before the end of the reporting period, March 31. This led to a lot of end-of-quarter scrambles to scrape together the cash for debtors who were in arrears. The Comptroller of the Currency finally put a stop to this—reportedly over the opposition of the Fed—and announced that the non-accrual deadline henceforth would be strictly enforced. As a result, most large U.S. banks reported lower earnings for the second quarter of 1984 because of non-receipt of interest on their Argentine loans. Because of Argentina's disagreement with the IMF over a stabilization program, the banks were not willing to put together a sufficiently large loan to cover the accumulated arrearages.

In the case of Poland, where the political situation precludes IMF or other official Western financial assistance, the banks in theory are insisting on full interest payment but have agreed to "relend" half. In effect, Poland is currently only paying half the interest due on its foreign bank debt. The advantage to the banks is that this arrangement allows them to show their Polish loans at full accrual with no reduction in the value of the asset.

Such repeated reschedulings and capitalization of interest have allowed the banks to pretend that sovereign risk lending is no-risk lending. Indeed, until the recent rule changes forced by Congress under the 1983 Act, one could look at the books of the major U.S. banks and not know there was a debt crisis, or a sharp deterioration in the quality of banks' foreign assets. If anything, these assets looked *more* valuable because many of them had been renegotiated at a higher rate of interest: They created an apparent improvement in the bank's "spread," the difference between the interest the bank paid for its money and the interest the bank received from borrowers.

Under the old rules, banks were expected to establish a loan-loss reserve against loans classified as "substandard" and "doubtful." Regulators have generally allowed bank management to decide the size and timing of such reserves, and practices have varied greatly from bank to bank. In recent years, the Internal Revenue Service has required that additions to such reserves be taken from post-tax earnings, which makes banks more reluctant to acknowledge loans as potential losses. When regulators classify a loan as a "loss," the affected bank has to write it off in whole or in part. The write-off is deducted from its loan-loss reserve and the reserve may then be replenished from current (pre-tax) earnings.

Loan-loss reserves at U.S. banks have increased in the last two years. The large "money-center" banks increased their average loan-loss reserves as a percentage of loans outstanding from 0.93 per cent in 1981 to 1.05 per cent at the end of 1983.[12] Since reserves are usually pooled rather than allocated by loan, it is hard to know how much of this is attributable to the foreign debt situation and how much to the rise in domestic bankruptcies, problems in the energy sector, and other domestic difficulties related to the 1981-83 recession. The annual reports of some banks make a rough allocation of the reserve against foreign and domestic loans; others do not. For example, at the end of 1983, Citicorp's reserve totaled $766 million, equal to 0.86 per cent of its outstanding loans of $88 billion. This is up from 0.79 per cent of loans in 1982. Citicorp's annual report does not indicate how much of the increase is due to international loan problems, but does state that an increase in write-offs in 1983 was "primarily related to debt servicing considerations on certain government and financial institutions lending," presumably mostly foreign. Chase Manhattan reports it increased the loan-loss reserve allocation for international loans from $275 million to $300 million, or 1.07 per cent of its foreign loans of $28 billion. The reserve allocation for domestic loans fell by $10 million. Although these marginal increments to reserves are welcome, many analysts believe that they still fall far short of what the banks may need on reserve to protect themselves against potential losses.

Interviews with bank regulators and with bankers indicate that although some private-sector loans to Latin America have been written down (partially written off) and more have been reserved against, many U.S. banks remain extremely reluctant to increase reserves or write down loans to foreign governments. Although West German banks, for example, have been required to write down their substantial Polish loans by 25 per cent each year for the past three years, until the recent rule changes many U.S. banks were carrying their Polish loans at full nominal value and had not reserved specifically against them. European banks are also reportedly partially writing off their Latin American loans, while most U.S. banks continue to insist that these are still good assets.

Under the 1983 Act, banks are required to establish special reserves (Allocated Transfer Risk Reserves, or ATRR)[13] for troubled foreign loans when such assets have been "impaired," as indicated by: (a) "a protracted inability of public or private borrowers in a foreign country to make payments on their external indebtedness," (b) the fact that "no definite prospects exist for the orderly restoration of debt service." These special reserves may not be pooled with other reserves or be considered capital. In addition, banks have to write down the asset by the amount of the reserve. That is, if a special reserve of 10 per cent is required, the "impaired" loans being reserved against will have to be shown on the books at 90 per cent rather than at 100 per cent of face value. In contrast, under the pooled reserve system banks increase their loan-loss provisions to reflect the total pool of substandard loans in their portfolios, but they may continue to carry such loans at full face value.

To ensure that the new rule is observed uniformly by all banking institutions, the Federal Financial Institutions Examination Council, composed of examiners from the three federal regulatory agencies, will decide which loans require an Allocated Transfer Risk Reserve, the timing and size of such a reserve, and whether an established ATRR may be reduced. The first year's reserve will normally be 10 per cent of the principal, with additional reserves in increments of 15 per cent per year if necessary. However, the banks are on notice that when a country has exhibited debt-service problems over several years, the initial reserve required may be substantially above 10 per cent.

Credits adversely affected by transfer risk will be classified as "substandard," "value impaired," and "loss." Loans will be classified as "value impaired" if more than one of the following is true: the country has not fully paid interest for six months; it has not complied with IMF adjustment programs; it has not met rescheduling terms for over one year; it shows no definite prospects for an orderly restoration of debt service in the near future. ATRRs will be required for loans classified as "value impaired." A bank may, however, opt to write down such loans by an equivalent amount and charge the write-down against its general loan-loss reserve, which must then be replenished out of current earnings. The net effect is the same—to force banks to increase reserves *and* to partially write off certain foreign loans.

Under the new rules, if the U.S. Treasury and several Latin neighbors had not put together an eleventh hour bail-out package for Argentina in March 1984, its loans would have been classified as "value impaired" and U.S. banks would have had to establish special reserves against loans to that country. At the time, Argentina had not paid interest on some loans for five months and was not even negotiating with the IMF. The government subsequently reduced interest arrearages to less than 90 days and began talks with the IMF.

As of the end of April 1984, ATRRs had been required only for Zaire, Sudan, Bolivia, Nicaragua, and Poland. Despite repeated and protracted debt-servicing interruptions in the first three cases, many U.S. banks apparently continued to show these loans as unimpaired assets. The reserve for Poland is 20 per cent and likely to rise because the regulators view the relending scheme as unsound—and perhaps because the U.S. government has no interest in making life easier for the Polish regime.

It is noteworthy that none of the large Latin American debtors is on the ATRR list, despite the fact that these are the borrowers that pose the biggest threat to the banks. In the summer of 1984, Brazil and Mexico appear to be in compliance with their IMF stabilization agreements and have made up interest arrearages on at least the public debt. But neither is paying principal and it is far too soon to say that these countries are now on sound financial footing. Neither Argentina nor Venezuela has an IMF agreement or a rescheduling agreement with the banks; Costa Rica is fighting with the IMF and has substantial interest arrearages and zero foreign-exchange reserves. Yet the criteria set forth by the regulators for deeming a loan "value impaired" are so narrow that no ATRR is required for any of these countries and banks may carry the loans at full nominal value if they so choose.

Another weakness of the new rule—one that illustrates an inherent conflict in the current dual role of regulators—is that new credits to "value impaired" countries are exempt from the ATRR requirement. The justification given is that under certain circumstances additional credit "may strengthen the functioning of the adjustment process, help to improve the quality of outstanding credit, and thus be consistent with the objectives of the program of improved supervision of international lending."[14] Thus the regulators are simultaneously trying to reduce the exposure of U.S.

banks through the ATRR and encouraging the banks to lend more—increasing their exposure—by exempting new loans. It seems that forcing the banks to accept significantly lower interest payments by certain troubled borrowers (instead of making new loans to enable the debtor to meet the current high interest charges) while at the same time beginning to write off some of the principal would be more consistent with the "objectives of. . .improved supervision of international lending" and would do more to solve the debt problem.

### Fees Charged by the Banks

In the 1983 Act, Congress also changed the rules on accounting for fees that banks charge on international loans. Critics had accused the banks of charging exorbitant fees on reschedulings and new emergency loans to beef up current earnings and thereby making the financial situation of troubled debtors even more difficult. There was also concern that, even under normal circumstances, large fees on regular loans that could be taken in as income immediately were an incentive for banks to lend when they should not have done so. Congress therefore decided that any loan fee exceeding the administrative or other specific cost of making a loan would have to be amortized over the life of the loan rather than taken in full up front. The first objective at least seems to have been met—in that banks appear more willing to waive or reduce fees for troubled debtors since the law was passed.

## International Cooperation

Better bank supervision in the United States is only half the battle. American banks are linked through interbank transactions, syndicated lending, and many other ties to thousands of foreign banks. National bank regulators are slowly coming to recognize that banks operating in the global credit market are interdependent, and that inadequate regulation and supervision of banks in one country can damage banks elsewhere. Failures such as those of Herstatt in West Germany and Banco Ambrosiano in Luxembourg can produce large losses for U.S. and other banks with whom they had interbank lines of credit or other business. Similarly, the quality of a U.S. bank loan to a foreign country can be affected by subsequent loans to that country by other financial institutions. And lack of cooperation from creditors in other countries can make country debt renegotiations difficult.

Recognition of a common interest in better supervision has not come easily. As mentioned earlier, the philosophical and structural approaches to bank supervision vary greatly from one country to another, even in Western Europe.[15] U.S. banks are subject to periodic inspection by government examiners; the United Kingdom relies on bank reporting and informal meetings with management; West Germany and Switzerland use private auditors to inspect banks. (In the mid-1970s, the same auditing firm was working for Citibank's Swiss entity and the Swiss banking authorities.) Some countries regulate only the parent bank while others look at banks on a consolidated, worldwide basis. Treatment of foreign branches and foreign subsidiaries varies in both host and home countries. Some authorities stress liquidity ratios, others look at capital adequacy, and there are no agreed standards for either. Disclosure requirements vary from country to country.

International cooperation among bank regulators did not begin because of concern over petrodollar recycling or the level of sovereign risk lending by banks. It was prompted by a series of bank failures involving foreign exchange speculation and/or fraud—that is, aberrant behavior by a few smaller banks that had serious repercussions on the whole banking system. In 1974, the Swiss subdivision of Britain's Lloyds Bank had foreign-exchange problems that threatened the parent. This was closely followed by the collapse of the Herstatt Bank in West Germany, which caused the interbank market to contract by 60 per cent and almost paralyzed the international payments system.[16] The Franklin National Bank also failed in 1974. Most recently, in 1983, there was the demise of Banco Ambrosiano's Luxembourg subsidiary.

The first important step toward an international approach to management of international banking was taken in September 1974, when the central bank governors of the Group of Ten countries (Belgium, Britain, Canada, France, Italy, Japan, Netherlands, Sweden, United States, and West Germany) plus Switzerland announced that they were prepared to provide adequate liquidity to the banking system in a crisis to prevent a repeat of the severe market contraction that had taken place after the Herstatt failure.

In December of that year, a second important step was taken when the Committee on Banking Regulation and Supervisory Practices was created under the auspices of the Bank for International Settlements (BIS) in Basel to begin bridging the differences in national supervision of international banking. This body, commonly referred to as the Cooke Committee of the Bank of England (after its current chairman, Peter Cooke) meets three or four times a year for two days. Because the Committee works on a consensus basis, there are few written agreements, though some reports on supervisory practices have been produced. Nevertheless, the Committee has brought about a "revolution in thinking," according to one long-time participant.

The Bank of England realized that Lloyds' Swiss entity had escaped supervision: The Swiss did not supervise it because it was a British bank and the British did not supervise it because it was located in Switzerland. When England broached the idea at an early meeting of the committee that all bank entities should be supervised by *someone*, the idea was not widely accepted. Nevertheless, by late 1975 the Cooke Committee had agreed (in the Basel Concordat) that all foreign bank establishments should be supervised and that parent and host authorities have a shared responsibility for supervising them. It was generally agreed that supervision (not provision) of solvency was the primary responsibility of the parent authorities in the case of branches and of the host authority in the case of subsidiaries. The supervision of liquidity is primarily up to the host authorities for both branches and subsidiaries. Although some countries still bar outside bank examiners, all members accept that there is an obligation to let the home supervisor know if a bank is getting into trouble in its jurisdiction. Participation in this early warning system was obviously a big step for countries protective of bank secrecy, such as Switzerland and Luxembourg. Still, the Concordat left some holes.

When Banco Ambrosiano's Luxembourg subsidiary collapsed, there was considerable disagreement about who was responsible for the supervisory failure and for picking up the pieces. Luxembourg is a party to the Basel Concordat, but not to the Group of Ten's lender-of-last-resort agreement. Because the subsidiary was technically an offshoot of an Ambrosiano non-bank holding company, it appeared not to be covered by the Concordat. Consequently, the Cooke Committee decided to update the 1975 agreement. The revised concordat makes clear that subsidiaries of holding companies are covered and are the primary responsibility of the host country, but that the parent authority must share responsibility and should ensure that the host is providing adequate supervision.

The revised concordat also endorses the idea that banks should have to keep their books on a consolidated basis, so that the home regulators can get a complete picture of a bank's global operations. The United States has required consolidation for some time, but other countries are moving ahead slowly, and there is still considerable resistance with regard to offshore operations in Panama, the Cayman Islands, and elsewhere.

The Bank for International Settlements has tried to gather uniform data on the foreign claims and liabilities of banks in participating countries, and its periodic reports are the best publicly available source of information on international banking. But the fragmented reporting by banks in some countries has left gaps. The non-consolidated Luxembourg subsidiaries of West German banks did most of the lending to Eastern Europe, for example; in German and BIS data, these loans show up as Luxembourg claims on Eastern Europe. French banks do not report foreign loans with maturities of less than two years. Because even the best available official data leaves gaps, the first step in rescheduling a country's foreign debt is usually a cumbersome polling of creditors around the world to determine who has loaned how much and on what terms. (Often the debtor does not know either.) Despite these remaining problems, consolidation should improve the quality of BIS data as well as bank supervision in participating countries.

The debt crisis has raised questions about the soundness of banks engaged in "normal" (as opposed to fraudulent or speculative) international banking. The Cooke Committee is focusing on capital adequacy as a measure of bank soundness and is trying to reach agreement on definitions of both capital and adequacy. Once these are agreed, capital adequacy would become a kind of international benchmark. However, the issue has become entangled in disagreements over how to deal with troubled foreign loans. The United States has stressed a gradual increase in capital as a way to strengthen banks, while some European countries have emphasized reducing assets by rapidly writing down troubled loans. Many European banks have "hidden" reserves—not shown on public reports—that may allow them to do this without cutting into dividends or current earnings. U.S. banks are prohibited from having hidden reserves; their current earnings are immediately affected by any write-down or increase in loan-loss reserves.

It has also become clear that certain countries in recent years abused the interbank market by having their own banks take billions of dollars in short-term placements from foreign banks and using these funds for medium-term balance-of-payments financing. In the case of Brazil, a number of U.S. banks have been dragooned into leaving several-day, one-week, three-week, and so on deposits with Banco do Brasil indefinitely while the government tries to work out of its debt squeeze. The Cooke Committee has discussed the problem of such abuses of the interbank market but has not agreed on a remedy. Some restrictions should be placed on the uses of the interbank market to prevent reliance on what is an essentially short-term market for medium-term balance-of-payments financing.

Clearly, international banking is no longer the exclusive domain of institutions from the industrial countries. In recent years,

Asian, Arab, and Latin American banks have claimed a significant share of the Euromarket. And even countries whose own banks are not active internationally play host to banks from the BIS group. The Cooke Committee has therefore begun inviting bank regulators from non-members to attend meetings for brief discussions of regulatory problems. One aim is to explain why foreign examiners might want to go poking around banks in those countries, and thereby ease access. A second objective is to strengthen bank supervision around the world. Some Third World countries have endorsed the Basel Concordat in principle but are not well equipped to supervise a rapidly growing domestic banking system or to closely monitor foreign banks in their jurisdiction. Some have started hiring bank-supervision consultants to help.

The mechanism now exists, albeit in a primitive state, for an international approach to international bank supervision. The Cooke Committee has taken important steps to increase oversight, information, and uniform treatment by national authorities and to bring into the process countries other than the industrial money centers. But the question is whether these measures go far enough or even address the most important questions. It is time that the Committee gave some thought to the possibility of supervising not just individual banks but the Eurocurrency market as a whole, to ensure that the rate of credit creation in the market is truly consistent with stable global economic expansion and that the instrumentalities used do not put debtors or creditors unnecessarily at risk.

The Committee should consider whether large syndicated country credits that are not linked to specific investments or commercial activities and are backed only by the general credit-standing of the borrowing country do constitute sound banking. Can banks judge the quality of a loan that is unrelated to a specific future income stream? And should the principal international commercial credit instrument continue to be the floating rate loan, which transfers the entire interest-rate risk from the lender to the borrower? Although this type of loan appears to limit the lender's risk, it may in fact increase the likelihood that the borrower will at some point experience debt-servicing difficulties because forces beyond the borrower's control can drive up interest rates. Recent regulatory reforms do not touch these issues, yet they are central to the current debt dilemma and the future shape of international lending.

The Cooke Committee should also take up the question of encouraging the growth of a secondary market for the existing stock of international loans that allows banks to reduce excessive exposures by selling off, at some real market price, the loans they no longer want to hold. One model for such arrangements is the secondary mortgage market in the United States.

## Conclusion

Recent regulatory changes in the United States mean that the international operations of U.S. banks will be subject to the same type—if not necessarily the same degree—of government regulation and supervision regarding safety and soundness as are their domestic operations. This recognizes that, for many regulatory purposes, the distinction between foreign and domestic banking is no longer meaningful.

Depositors, stockholders, and potential investors will know much more about what banks are doing abroad. The increased transparency of foreign operations should by itself restrain banks from repeating some of the lending excesses of the past. Uniform and more stringent rules regarding asset classification, loan-loss reserves, and capital ratios should bring an element of realism to a system of bookkeeping of foreign loans that had been largely based on fantasy and wishful thinking. Mistakes will have to be acknowledged and the penalties paid. This, too, will have a disciplinary effect on future bank operations as well as strengthening banks in dealing with their current crop of troubled international loans.

If rigorously enforced, these rule changes would appear to make life tougher for debtor countries. As the highly complex bailout of Argentina's creditors in March 1984 demonstrated, the new U.S. banking rules make it more difficult to finesse the periodic interruptions of debt servicing by Latin American and other debtor countries. More banks are likely to defect from the bank/government/IMF rescue packages that involve lending new money to countries that cannot keep up interest payments. That sleight of hand can no longer be used by banks to escape recognizing the old loans as impaired assets. Even countries with a good record of debt servicing may have a harder time securing bank credit because firm capital ratios will put a cap on more international lending by some banks if the stock markets take a highly negative view of their existing exposures. If banks cannot sell shares (increase equity), they will not be allowed to increase assets.

Debtors should perhaps also be concerned that the IMF's role in bestowing the "Good Housekeeping seal of approval" to countries' adjustment programs is now enshrined in U.S. banking legislation. Since failure by a country owing money to U.S. banks to negotiate or live up to IMF agreements can trigger certain penalties for the banks, debtor countries may have even less leverage in negotiating with the Fund. (It is of course possible that the legislation could have the opposite effect—that banks and the U.S. government would side with the debtor and pressure the IMF to yield in negotiations in order to produce an agreement.)

Does this mean that the recent regulatory reforms will make the debt crisis worse? No. But if enforced—and the stock market will react negatively if it appears that they are not—the rules will press adoption of a different approach to the crisis, one that shifts more of the costs to the banks. Enough new money will not be available to cover interest payments, and banks will either have to negotiate interest concessions or accept unilateral reductions in payments by the debtors. Current earnings would be lost. For example, if in 1983 the nine large U.S. money-center banks had received only half the interest due from the nine largest developing-country debtors (assuming an across-the-board 14 per cent rate on their total reported claims on these countries), their total pre-tax income for the year would have fallen from $6.5 billion to about $2.8 billion.[17] On the other hand, banks would not have to continue putting new money into countries whose ability to pay is already in doubt. And debtors would gain some cash flow relief without seeing their total indebtedness continue to rise merely for the purpose of paying interest on old debts.

There are those who believe this would not necessarily be a bad thing.

## Notes

[1] The term "regulation" is here used in its broader sense, meaning the various forms of intervention by government banking authorities. In the United States, the main regulatory agencies at the national level are the Federal Reserve (state-chartered bank members of the Fed system), the Comptroller of the Currency (nationally chartered banks), and the Federal Deposit Insurance Corporation (state-chartered, insured, non-Fed member banks). Fed and FDIC jurisdictions overlap somewhat with state banking authorities.

Regulators distinguish between "regulation" and "supervision." The first refers to specific rules, dos and don'ts that apply uniformly to all banks and types of bank. The latter refers to the more ad hoc guidance given by the regulatory agencies to banks on an individual basis. Thus bank examiners are given certain guidelines as to what constitutes safe and sound banking practices, but have considerable leeway in applying them to specific cases. What may be unsafe and unsound for Bank A may be perfectly all right for Bank B, which has a different portfolio, capital, and reserve structure, etc. The U.S. system is a combination of regulation and supervision. Certain countries, England for example, emphasize supervision over regulation. Some so-called offshore banking centers have for all intents and purposes neither regulation nor supervision.

[2] "Volcker Defends Bank Interests," *Washington Post*, April 5, 1984, p. B-1.

[3] The subsequent explosive growth of the Eurocurrency market was not directly linked to U.S. trade deficits but was fueled by dollar placements from OPEC, U.S. residents, and others and by the credit creation of the market itself. Economists disagree about the precise growth mechanism.

[4] See "Multinational Banks and U.S. Foreign Policy," Hearings of the Subcommittee on Multinational Corporations, Committee on Foreign Relations, U.S. Senate, Part

15, July 16, September 11 and 18, and October 9 and 29, 1975 (Washington, D.C.: U.S. Government Printing Office, 1976).

[5] Testimony by Anthony Solomon, Under Secretary for Monetary Affairs, Department of the Treasury, "The Witteveen Facility and the OPEC Financial Surpluses," Hearings of the Subcommittee on Foreign Economic Policy, Committee on Foreign Relations, U.S. Senate, September 21, 1977 (Washington, D.C.: U.S. Government Printing Office, 1978).

[6] "A New Supervisory Approach to Foreign Lending," Federal Reserve Bank of New York, *Quarterly Review*, Spring 1978, pp. 1-6.

[7] In the language of bank accounting, a bank's *assets* are (primarily) its loans (i.e., its claims on other parties); a bank's *liabilities* are its deposits, equity, and funds borrowed from other banks (i.e., other parties' claims on the bank). Banks lend liabilities to create assets.

[8] The peculiar grouping of banks in the Country Risk Lending Survey—"nine largest banks," "next fifteen largest"—is a historical accident. The Survey grew out of an effort by the Senate Foreign Relations Committee in 1975 to get data on the claims and liabilities of U.S. banks. The committee wanted the information on a bank-by-bank basis and sent out a questionnaire. The bigger banks protested vigorously and a compromise was worked out whereby the Fed would collect the data and provide it to the committee in three-bank aggregates, grouped by size (three biggest, and so on). This would protect the confidentiality of individual bank relations with individual governments. The banks were particularly concerned about the prospects that the size of their Arab deposits would be divulged. Grouping the banks by threes, it was thought, would protect them. When the Fed got the data, however, it discovered that the petrodollar deposits were so highly concentrated in the top three banks that it would be potentially embarrassing to the banks and their Arab clients to release even this aggregate number.

[9] Henry C. Wallich, "International Commercial Banking from a Central Bank Viewpoint," Federal Reserve Board, December 29, 1983.

[10] William R. Cline, *International Debt and the Stability of the World Economy* (Washington, D.C.: Institute for International Economics, 1983), p. 36.

[11] Ibid.

[12] Bank Securities Department, Salomon Brothers, Inc., *A Review of Bank Performance: 1984 Edition* (New York: 1984), Figure 23, p. 39.

[14] Statement issued by the Board of Governors of the Federal Reserve System, February 8, 1984.

[15] For a survey of regulatory practices in the major industrial countries, see Richard Dale, "Bank Supervision Around the World," Group of Thirty, New York, N.Y., 1982.

[16] See Karin Lissakers, "A Bank Crash by New Year's Eve?," *Washington Post*, November 21, 1982.

[17] Author's calculations. Based on bank earnings reports.

Chapter 3

# The Role of Information: Closing the Barn Door?

Christine A. Bogdanowicz-Bindert and
Paul M. Sacks

With the eruption of the debt crisis, the way commercial banks assess sovereign risk has come under heavy criticism. One common theme has been the absence of "good" information about developing countries, and the belief that had such information been available to lenders in the first place, the debt crisis might not have occurred.

Acting on this assumption, the major U.S. commercial banks reached into their pockets to fund an experiment, the Institute of International Finance (IIF), which was "created as a center for the dissemination of information to member organizations, borrowing countries, multilateral organizations and regulators, *in order to improve the process of international lending...*" (authors' emphasis). Similar motives prompted the Japanese, with the help of various government agencies, to create the Japan Center for International Finance (JCIF).

This chapter considers whether "good" information is key to sound international lending by commercial banks. The analysis is based on a series of case studies of money-center and regional banks, conducted over the last year, as well as the professional experience of both authors, which includes advising commercial banks and developing countries on a wide range of economic, political, and financial issues.

During the lending boom of the 1970s, information analysts felt they were voices clamoring in the wilderness. Today's more cautious lending environment makes them feel their analyses really matter. In the years ahead, however, the role of information in lending decisions will depend more on market forces than on anything banks will have learned from the current experience. Although much has and can be done to improve information quality and use, the critical variables influencing the banks' international behavior, loan allocation, and pricing are their external environment, the internal structure of the organization, and the extent of their international exposure.

Banks, in other words, are merely a special kind of organization; they respond to their particular environment in much the same ways as other large organizations. Some are better positioned to react to environmental sea changes than others. Banking institutions in the United States are a particular subset—different in how they relate to government, regulators, the size of the domestic market, the domestic equity market in which their senior management must survive, and the international markets in which they operate. For instance, U.S. banks have been particularly inflexible on the issue of interest rates in debt reschedulings because of their concern about bank regulators and shareholders. Another constraint within which they operate is the need to maintain quarterly earnings, which has inhibited their ability to take a longer-term view of the current debt crisis.

Thus the responsibility for the banks' international behavior should not be laid at the feet of only one part of the organization: the country-risk analyst.

## Setting Country Limits: Approaches of Major U.S. Banks in the 1970s

The "softness" of sovereign risk analysis during the 1970s was not linked to a lack of information but to the use of available information by the lending banks. The behavior of banks as evidenced by their loan allocation and pricing decisions was less in response to the actual economic performance of a given sovereign borrower than to factors such as the overall lending environment and each bank's organizational characteristics.

The reason for the relatively small weight given to information in establishing the creditworthiness of a sovereign borrower is a compound one. It can be described in terms of stages in the information gathering, analysis, and decision-making process. First, the analysis of available information by bank country-risk, credit, and lending officers during the pre-debt-crisis period left much to be desired. Second, the extent to which this information was "utilized" in lending decisions during this period was circumscribed by several factors, not the least of which was the substantial autonomy of lending officers during the era of recycling enthusiasm.

The main vehicle for increased international lending to sovereign creditors was the syndicated credit, in which financial exposure and risk were spread among several participating banks. During the 1970s, the number of institutions participating in loan syndications increased more than tenfold. This meant that many small- and medium-sized banks, with little or no previous experience in sovereign lending, became active in the market.

The new participants relied almost exclusively on the money-center banks, which were responsible for arranging the syndicated credits. The primary source of information for these new participants was the information or "placement" memorandum in which a country's economic and political situation was described. These memoranda were usually compiled by bank syndication departments, often with the support of economists, on the basis of statistics collected in the debtor country and information published by multilateral organizations such as the International Monetary Fund, the World Bank, and the Bank for International Settlements (BIS). In some cases, confidential memoranda prepared by regional development banks (such as the Inter-American Development or African Development Banks), the World Bank, or the IMF were also used.

The risk analysis done at the large money-center banks differed both in form and content from that provided to newly participating institutions, however. The internal documents prepared at the money-center banks were much more elaborate, detailed, and candid than the information memoranda used to make the sales pitch associated with a loan syndication. Part of the difference was due to restrictions placed by bank legal departments on what could be published in the placement memoranda because they were afraid there would be some legal responsibility if banks went beyond actual history and facts in judging a country's credit viability. Although many regional banks were aware of these limitations, the strength of the lending impulse induced myopia in many.

Clearly, the content and quality of the banks' information memoranda were more critical in the decision processes of regional banks than of the money centers. Viewed objectively, the memoranda were written as sales documents (and, to a lesser extent, for bank regulators) and were primarily intended as a formality. They served to pave the way for a decision that was in large part already taken: to increase international exposure.

The difficulties with these memoranda commenced with well-known problems at the source—the absence of timely, accurate, and full information about borrowing countries. These problems were compounded, however, when the information reached the threshold of lending institutions. The data and analysis provided in placement memoranda were often an inadequate basis on which to form a lending decision, as the memoranda tended to be primarily descriptive and retrospective.

The imperfections of the information memoranda themselves were not the only reason for the problems besetting bank risk analysis. The shortcomings had more to do with the broad context in which the memoranda were done.

Throughout the bull market years of the 1970s, the role of the risk analyst was marginal; the force of the recycling impulse not only overrode risk considerations but also influenced loan allocation and pricing decisions. Pushed by the heavy inflows of petrodollar deposits and pulled by the rising developing-country demand for the funding of ambitious development projects and chronic current-account deficits, commercial banks aggressively pursued international lending activities. As a result, non-oil developing countries and the Eastern bloc countries increased their indebtedness to banks sevenfold between 1971 and 1982.

The incentive for biased judgment was very great. First, there was stiff competition from other lending institutions. Furthermore, banks were structured in such a way that within each organization there was a strong bias in favor of lending. The economist usually had a limited role in the decision process and the loan officer's performance was measured by his "salesmanship" quality.

Although the approach to credit-risk analysis varied from bank to bank, the most prevalent system used in the 1970s was a standardized country evaluation report with a narrowly defined scope, accompanied by some statistics. Few banks reviewed the accuracy of their initial forecast against the country's actual economic performance, and thus did not assess the reliability of their method of credit-risk analysis. Finally, it seems that no bank explicitly used its country rating system in fixing the level of spreads and fees. Rather, banks that had developed internal rating systems used these primarily for the analysis of extant portfolios, namely the assessment of existing exposures and the extent that these corresponded to the degree of "risk."

In summary: The country information that was available within the money-center banks was flawed; even had it been "good" information, it would not have diverted the major money-center banks from a course largely directed by the pressures of excess liquidity and increased competition. The information made available to new participants in the sovereign lending market in the 1970s was usually cast within the context of what was intended as a sales document, the placement memorandum. At the peak of the recycling process, international sovereign lending was not considered a problem. As a result, sovereign lending decision processes had few built-in checks and balances in the 1970s.

## Limiting Country Exposure: The Rescheduling Era of the 1980s

Since the eruption of the debt crisis and widespread rescheduling exercises, the banks' herd instinct has prompted a 180-degree switch to a strong lending bias against developing countries. To be sure, some additional lending has occurred, but on an involuntary basis. The money-center banks have been willing to go along with "muddling through" by providing new money, while the regional banks, following their own herd instinct, have been far more reluctant to participate in this process. The changes in the international environment have been paralleled by improvements in the quality and use of country-risk analysis by all segments of the international lending community.

### Staff Adaptations

In reaction to the changing international lending environment, the role of country-risk analysts—defined broadly to include economists as well as credit and political analysts—has been enhanced and changed in focus. The major broadening of responsibilities has involved a greater influence over loan allocation as banks become more responsive to risk considerations.

At the money-center banks, staff economists have had their workload dramatically increased as they have stretched themselves between traditional lending exercises—where less lending does not necessarily translate into less work—and the additional burden of staffing new rescheduling structures (new units within their own bank as well as interbank economic committees). In addition, as a result of a process that commenced during the mid-1970s, the number of country-risk analysts has grown. A significant development within this trend has been the addition of professional political analysts, whose primary function is to assess a country's willingness to repay its debts and to assist economists in their analysis of how public policies affect that country's capacity to repay. Well over half the major money-center banks now employ such professional political analysts. It should be noted, however, that most of these specialists were hired immediately prior to the onset of the debt crisis.

A special problem or paradox has emerged as a result of these staffing changes: The expertise appropriate to the bull market of the 1970s has been too geographically dispersed to cope with the concentration of problems in Latin America and Eastern Europe. Thus many institutions do not have enough specialists on Latin America and Eastern Europe, and they are unwilling to add additional personnel while international profits are down. Consequently, just when country-risk analysts are becoming better "positioned" to offset the lending bias, the rigidities of the staffing process have left their departments unable to adapt properly.

Among the regional banks, few increases in staff have occurred. But the influence of risk analysts has increased vis-à-vis loan officers. Moreover, as a result of the tensions that have emerged between the regional and the money-center banks, regional risk analysts have sought to rely less on the money-center banks for their information. Contrary to expectations, the regional banks have not joined the new Institute of International Finance in the numbers originally hoped for by its money-center bank founders. (According to the IIF, only 34 U.S. regionals had joined as of May 31, 1984.) The reasons for this reluctance range from radically reduced amounts of international activity to a perception that the IIF is little more than a thinly disguised big-bank institution. The regionals' major new sources of information now include a variety of independent assessments, such as their own direct connections with borrowing countries and outside consultants.

## Information

Since the level of voluntary lending has declined precipitously and since most of the new money is currently associated with rescheduling packages, the bulk of the information and analysis provided by commercial banks now focuses on the crisis in each country and on its resolution. Information memoranda are still used as the basic documents, but they are supplemented by much more detailed information—analyses of reasons for the crisis, the ongoing economic and financial situation, the measures taken by the government to address the crisis, and alternative scenarios for the country's future. These scenarios are based on the impact of domestic policies as well as on assumptions about exogenous variables such as growth in industrial countries, outlook for interest rates, and prices for key commodities. In addition, IMF documents are more widely distributed than in the past, as they are now typically requested from the debtor by the Steering Committee (made up of the banks selected to lead the rescheduling negotiation). In short, the quality and quantity of information available to lenders has markedly improved.

The banks have also started to do more digging in areas previously not really explored in information memoranda. This probing includes detailed questioning on the future outlook for the country's economic and financial situation, measures that authorities plan to introduce to cope with current difficulties, the extent to which economic measures can be pushed through the political system, detailed analysis of the foreign-exchange cash flow and balance-of-payments situation, and a more realistic appraisal than in the past of the sources of financing.

Those banks with smaller international portfolios are still unable to match the analytic depth of the money-center banks. For example, even for a major debtor such as Mexico, no major U.S. bank devotes a full-time person to follow current economic developments. Needless to say, the degree of effort devoted to monitoring the implementation of the rescheduling package of a smaller debtor like Costa Rica, for example, is necessarily limited. Nowhere in the world of commercial banking does the specialization and division of labor characterizing public-sector bureaucracies exist.

## Institutional Responses and Decision Structures

Interestingly enough, a review of the process by which banks collect information and make decisions points up that no two systems are identical. Each bank has responded to the changing international lending environment distinctively, reflecting the constraints of its particular situation. More importantly, however, the disparity indicates that no bank has achieved a significant "breakthrough" in the way it evaluates sovereign creditworthiness that would induce other institutions to follow suit.

Although banks responded differently to the change in the international environment, the clear trend has been to develop more defensive postures toward international lending—in contrast to the 1970s, when all new international lending opportunities tended to be regarded favorably. The "defensiveness" of the post-debt crisis environment is characterized by an initially negative attitude to the word "international." The organizational consequence of this attitude has been to involve all parts of the international lending structure, in addition to the loan officer, in new lending and rescheduling decisions.

Internally, however, the nature of defensive mechanisms varies. The differences observed in the case studies done were a function of three factors: the bank's institutional character, the balance between line and staff officers, and the size of its international exposure.

First, each bank's institutional character influenced its response to the debt crisis. How it revised its country-limits process was affected by such factors as the degree of centralization or the extent to which a bank was organized along either functional or geographic lines. For instance, where banks had mainly relied on a key senior decision maker to determine final lending limits, introduction of a more open, pluralistic process has proved difficult. Alternatively, where all the senior management had involved itself extensively in country lending decisions, the more defensive environment has accentuated this process; in one major bank, the committee that sets exposure limits literally consists of the very top management of the bank, as opposed to the more typical situation where the level of decision making corresponds to the amounts involved. In general, the new international environment has resulted in a more layered, pluralistic process.

The second major difference observed was the balance between line and staff officers in the decision process. The separation between those who "make money" (the line people) and those who "cost money" (the economist, political scientist, and credit analyst) greatly influenced the extent to which staff analysts were able to offset the bank's lending bias. Recently, staff have become much more integrated into the decision process, and lending officers less dominant. Country-risk analysts are "listened to" more in the defensive environment; previously the bull market for international lending drowned out their cautionary pleas. The bear market has thus had internal consequences on the politics of country-risk information and has opened the decision process to more players.

Third, the size of a bank's international exposure continues to influence its role as information gatherer and provider. In the past, greater international activity roughly correlated with the size of international staff. Today, banks with large exposures in "problem" developing countries are more actively involved in the rescheduling process, particularly through their participation on Steering Committees. This translates into more intimate knowledge of problem countries. In addition, they are devoting a large portion of time to disseminating this information to other banks, as well as trying to persuade them to put fresh money into these countries.

In sum, the information and decision process in international lending has been altered by the debt crisis. In particular, the role of risk analysts, the information gathered by them, and the use of this information has changed substantially over the past two years. Risk analysis of course remains an art with significant room for improvement. Even so, there will continue to be limits on the extent to which informational "fixes" will diminish the force of markets over individual lending decisions.

## What More Can Be Done?

As long as a more defensive international lending environment prevails, changes in information flows and decision processes are unlikely to be reversed. What, then, is the most appropriate way to organize the flow of information to the decision makers? And, more important, how can banks avoid falling back into the lending bias trap at the next upswing in international lending?

Some banks may well conclude that the era of voluntary international lending has come to a close—that maintaining a large risk-assessment team is not cost-effective—and will focus their efforts primarily on trade and project financing. This would be an error. The experience of the past several years has proved that the line between short-term trade financing and longer-term lending is in practice a blurry one, and that earmarked project finance funds and balance-of-payments loans are all too often co-mingled. And Latin America and Africa, where most reschedulings have been concentrated, are only part of the world. International lending continues in Europe, Asia, much of the Middle East, Australia, and New Zealand. Finally, regulators will demand more due diligence with regard to international lending. Thus the information requirements of the 1980s are likely to be more stringent than some bankers currently believe.

Banks need to build a country-risk system based on the more defensive lending environment of the 1980s and try to ensure maximum openness of the information system that feeds the exposure-setting process. The key to a better credit-risk analysis system is to promote constructive debate at all levels of the decision-making process. Some banks have already introduced parallel or duplicate streams of country information, where the staff work at headquarters either complements or replicates line and/or field reports. Such systems are more likely to highlight any disagreements and hence to avoid any major oversight. The decision process should be totally open, enabling anybody to "rock the boat," and economists, political scientists, and credit analysts should be given equal weight in the decision process with line people.

The energy devoted to econometric modeling could well be redirected into applying the insights of organization theory to international lending decisions.

Banks should resist relying on other lending institutions for information and assessments related to sovereign lending, and instead seek ways to enhance their self-confidence. This suggestion is aimed mainly at the regional banks, but it applies to several of the major banks as well. One way to implement it is to integrate alternative analysis from independent sources into the institution's decision process. Over the past two years, in fact, the number of independent sources of analysis (country-risk consulting firms and special institutes) has grown dramatically.

Finally, some effort should be made to preserve this more open and adversarial process even in the event of a more competitive international lending climate. Indeed, if a lesson can be drawn from the excesses of the 1970s, it is that risk considerations should not be allowed to govern international lending.

Improvements such as these in the international lending process will not, of course, prevent banks from making some loans that are not justified on economic or financial grounds. Many international loans are made because of a long-standing relationship between the debtor and its creditors. But banks have a reputation for short memories, and a defense mechanism should be built into the decision process now to assure that the next lending upswing is not the last.

# Chapter 4

# Foreign Banks in the Domestic Markets of Developing Countries

George J. Clark

International banks have very large dollar portfolios with domestic borrowers in the developing countries. A great deal has been written about this "cross-border" exposure in international or "hard" currencies, which currently totals some $400 billion. Yet there is another important aspect of international bank activity in the domestic financial markets of the developing countries that is much less commonly reported upon. This is the purely domestic (i.e., local-currency) commercial banking business performed within these markets by the international banks. These activities are performed through local branches and local subsidiaries (wholly or partly owned) of many of the major international banks. Some of these operations are now over one hundred years old, although most of their growth has taken place in the last twenty-five years or so.

In addition to branches and subsidiaries, the international banking community often maintains representative offices within the developing countries. These offices do not, however, have sources of local funds and consequently do not lend in local currencies. Representative offices perform the function of managing locally the "cross-border" portfolio and therefore, strictly speaking, are not a part of the domestic banking market. Similarly, the major international banks also maintain friendly service relations with local "correspondent" banks, but this activity is more appropriately considered within the "cross-border" category, since most transactions are in other than domestic currencies.

## Reasons for International Bank Involvement

The origin of the involvement of the large international banks in the local banking markets is closely linked to the multinational corporate clients of those banks. As these international clients, located in the key capitals of the world, developed their overseas sources of raw materials and markets for their goods, they created a need for banking services in the local markets. In the first instance, this need related to the opening of letters of credit for the local supplier of raw materials, or for the local purchase of the products of the international clients. The ability of the local banks to open these letters of credit was not highly developed, and consequently the international client often appealed to counterparts in the head office of the home "correspondent" banks to try to perform this service locally.

Over time, the need to open letters of credit was extended to the need for local-currency financing in order to enable the local client to purchase the goods of the international client—or to buy raw materials locally and stock them for later purchase by the international firm. This latter development meant the local bank needed to develop a local source of funds. In many of these markets, an interbank source of funds did not exist, and therefore money could not be bought outright. In such circumstances, the international banks were driven to open branch networks in order to take deposits in local currency. This necessitated the development of a full-service local banking business by the international banks.

In its earlier phases, much of this activity was associated with colonialism; British banks tended to do the local banking business in British colonies, and French banks were to be found in the French colonies. During the period between the two world wars, this approach weakened significantly. Banks of several nationalities were established in some of the more important local banking markets. The pace of this process increased rapidly after about 1960. Nevertheless, such vestiges of the colonial system remain significant in some parts of the world.

Although it is true that this local banking initiative was originally undertaken by the international banking community in support of its major corporate clients, the international banks came to realize over the years that this line of business could stand on its own merits. Local banking, if well done, could be profitable in its own right. Indeed, the characteristics of some markets were sufficiently favorable so that the international banks' earnings in these local markets could, and often did, achieve returns superior to those to be found in the markets of the head offices. Thus the importance of the international clients to the international banks was superseded over time by that of the purely local client base. In more recent years, domestic lending by international banks in developing-country markets has tended to grow rapidly—simply because the local markets often presented better profitability characteristics than were to be found at home.

## Advantages and Drawbacks to Host Nations

As the local bank business of the international banks has developed over time, the host governments have been called upon to ponder in depth the advantages and drawbacks of this activity. In spite of the perception that a large international bank operating locally would have many advantages over the relatively smaller domestic banks, the fact is that very rarely did the international banks become major players in the local markets. They tended to avoid the labor- and cost-intensive programs involved in the development of large local branch systems. They generally operated relatively few principal branches in the major cities, and their client base tended to be limited to urban non-mass markets. Almost everywhere the extensive local branch networks were owned either by the local government or by the local business community. This situation had many advantages from the point of view of the local regulators—because the market share of the international banks was consequently rarely more than 5 per cent. For this relatively small market share, the country had a contact with the main office of a large international bank—with all that might imply in terms of the introduction of modern systems and technologies. Yet most of the domestic banking activity remained in the hands of domestic owners.

International banks may increase the efficiency of the domestic market—either by making it more competitive or by making it more efficient. A 1979 U.S. Treasury Department report suggests that the international banks would benefit from having discriminatory practices against them in the local banking markets eliminated; but the report emphasizes that the domestic economies would likewise gain in the process, through increased competition and heightened efficiency. The report also points out that restrictions impose opportunity costs on the international banks precisely in the area where the domestic market would also bear the highest cost.[1] Some wise governments have used these insights to encourage international bank activities in their markets. A recent example has been Japan's efforts to encourage international banks to make consumer loans in order to reduce the inefficiencies and high costs of local lenders, the "Sarakins." There are reasons to believe that the current Australian government may be thinking in similar terms.

From the host government's point of view, the principal drawback of an international banking presence is probably the negative reactions of domestic groups. The local banking community is certain to perceive the large international banks as being interlopers who have unfair advantages in the domestic competition for business. In fact, the international banks do enjoy advantages—just as they suffer disadvantages—but the fact that their global base is broader and their head office is located abroad makes them vulnerable to domestic criticism from competing forces. The struggle between localism and internationalism continues in most markets, with some years being characterized by more liberal approaches and other years by increased restrictions.

The local activities of the international banks also pose some problems for the local regulators. For example, a local branch of an international bank may operate without any local capital, since the capital of the total bank is available to support the activities of the local branch. Nevertheless, local regulators often feel the need for the local branch to have its own capital base, in which case there is a capital redundancy from the point of view of the international bank's head office.

The typical way to handle these conflicting points of view is compromise. The international banks often are required to operate under special restrictions, such as a limit on the number of branches, a limit on share of the market, requirements to have local partners, or special capital requirements. These restrictions reflect the local pressures that are exerted upon the regulators, and they raise the question of whether the structure is changing. In fact, it is very difficult to discern a trend line toward either heightened or lessened restrictions on these international banks. For example, recent trends in the Middle East have pointed toward increasing restrictions on the international banks (such as the "Saudization" program in Saudi Arabia) while the Latin markets, on the other hand, have tended to pull back somewhat from earlier restriction efforts. The specific examples cited might suggest that countries increasingly dependent upon the international banks for dollar loans may be more cautious in imposing restrictions, while surplus dollar areas feel no such constraints. In fact, it is probably true that governments do, to some extent, take into consideration their foreign-currency needs when considering restrictions on the international banks. A recent specific example is the Republic of Korea, which liberalized its two-way credit ("swapping") arrangements in 1980 when foreign exchange was critically short.

## Relationship Between Local Involvement and "Cross-Border" Banking

A subtle relationship exists between local and cross-border banking activities. International banks like to feel that the local presence that comes about through involvement in substantial local commercial banking activities provides insights and understandings about the country situation that enhance the ability of the international bank to evaluate its own cross-border position. The local presence involves extensive local staffing and close working relationships with government officials and key clients in the local economy. These relationships should provide much useful intelligence regarding attitudes and opportunities that are important in evaluating country risk. An international bank with a substantial local presence should be "among the first to know" when significant changes in attitudes and opportunities are taking place.

However, this situation is not without its own downsides. Local banking activities can easily be restricted by local authorities, and even the largest international bank has great difficulty in dealing with local regulators if those regulators take a position contrary to the perceived interest of the international bank. (Thus President Allende, for example, had no difficulty in eliminating international banks from Chile in his first year in office.) It is not unknown in international banking for local authorities to put pressure on international banks to "save the franchise" at times when their central bank would like the international banks to provide more foreign exchange.

It is conceivable that developing countries may offer to liberalize restrictions on international banks, or to permit additional entry for international banks as these countries seek to regain their access to international capital markets. In practice, however, this hypothetical possibility does not seem to be significant, at least under today's market conditions. The "involuntary" packages that have been put together since the Mexican crisis of 1982 involve a *pro rata* allocation of additional cross-border exposure for all international banks having exposure in the country. Consequently, it has been difficult for the lending bank, and unnecessary for the developing country, to suggest that some special advantage might be offered to an individual international bank as a *quid pro quo* for making additional loans available.

## Remittability of Domestic Earnings

A major distinction needs to be drawn regarding the earnings of international banks on their cross-border exposure and on their local-currency business. Cross-border exposure is compensated by payments in international currencies. However, local-currency business generates earnings in local currency. Equity accounting permits the international banks to take into their earnings these local-currency earnings when generated even if those earnings are not converted into foreign exchange. Even so, commercial banks do need to explain to their auditors how ultimate convertibility will be achieved. This raises the question of the convertibility of local earnings—a consideration that is obviously particularly critical at this time, when foreign-exchange availability is limited in most developing countries.

Foreign-exchange restrictions have often impeded remittability of local-currency earnings of the international banks. Consequently international banks entering into this line of activity face the very real additional risk that their local activities will be successful, but that the result of the success will be specifically reduced or wiped out as unremitted profits accumulate and lose purchasing power through inflation and devaluation. Further risk derives from the fact that the local government, anxious to hold on to available foreign exchange, often taxes heavily any remittance of local earnings.

However, with respect to loss of value through inflation, banks are in a particularly favorable position to protect themselves. Protection may take the form of investment in real assets (banking offices, real estate, etc.), which provide a good hedge against inflation. Since international banks typically operate only in major urban centers, their investments in real estate have proved to be quite successful in the postwar period, especially because of rapid urbanization in the developing world. Moreover, unremitted earnings represent a source of funding for the local branch of the international bank. With good financial management, these funds can be lent out or otherwise appropriately invested so as to maintain their foreign-exchange purchasing power. In this way, the real value of local earnings will be maintained until remittance once again becomes possible. Finally, with respect to taxes on remittances, many home governments permit local taxes to be applied against head-office taxes—with the net effect being that the international bank pays more taxes locally and fewer taxes at home. Therefore, the remittance tax may not increase the bank's total tax bill.

For these reasons, the postwar record on overseas earnings for the international banks has not been greatly affected by the limited availability of foreign exchange. By and large the delayed remittability of local earnings has not tended to be the major obstacle for international banks operating at the local level that many observers had predicted.

## Policy Recommendations for Developing-Country Governments

Traditional views regarding the effectiveness of free markets would suggest that minimum restrictions on the international banks are probably in the interest of the developing countries. On the one hand, local operations by international banks provide an additional source of financial strength, and innovative systems and modern technologies that can expedite the process of improving the quality of the local banking system. On the other hand, the record clearly shows that, almost without exception, the domestic banking system has been able to maintain its predominant position in the local financial market. Developing-country officials and regulators continually need to be reminded of this fact in order for them to be more at ease with free access by the international banks to the domestic markets.

If restrictions are felt to be needed, they should not take the form of restrictions on entry or restrictions to access of local funds. Probably the most effective type of restriction is to limit the number of banking locations (as has been done in Greece and Turkey). After all, the technology and system leadership that the international banks can provide is readily demonstrable with even a few locations for banking activities.

## Policy Recommendations for the U.S. Government

In dealing with foreign governments regarding international banking, the United States uses the principle of "national treatment," whereby, to the extent reasonably possible, international banks are subject to the same restrictions and have the same privileges as domestic banks. This concept was enacted into law in the International Banking Act of 1978, whereby branches of foreign banks are guaranteed the right to operate within the United States with the same restrictions and privileges as domestic banks. In spite of these efforts there are still countries in which international banks do not, in fact, enjoy national treatment (for example, Australia, Canada, and Taiwan). By and large the United States has not taken an active role in trying to adjust these discrepancies.

Consequently, it may now become increasingly relevant to think in terms of introducing aspects of reciprocity, as distinct from national treatment, into the regulatory process. Under conditions of reciprocity, U.S. operations of foreign banks would be restricted if the operations of U.S. banks in the foreign country were in some way restricted beyond the restrictions imposed by the host country on its own commercial banks. An example of reciprocity arrangements is illustrated by current New York State law, which permits foreign banks to establish branches within New York City, provided that New York banks are allowed entry into the entering bank's home country. This type of legislation may have been useful in encouraging the Canadians to reconsider the restrictions they place in terms of share of market on foreign banks operating in Canada. Senator Garn has indicated that he will hold hearings in this regard because of some clear examples of discrimination in some local markets against international banks.

It may be possible to think in terms of a compromise between the issues of reciprocity and national treatment. This might involve "reciprocal national treatment," entailing a review by U.S. federal regulators before approval of any new activity of a foreign bank. The regulators would be charged by federal law to review the extent to which there is, in fact, national treatment for U.S. commercial banks operating in foreign countries when foreign banks of those countries seek to avail themselves of national treatment in the U.S. market. In the approval process, the regulators might weigh the extent to which U.S. banks do not receive national treatment in the country applying for new activities. A current example might be an application by a Swedish bank to operate in U.S. markets under the International Banking Act. Such additional discipline would of course require new legislation, as an amendment to the International Banking Act.

## Notes

[1] See U.S. Department of the Treasury, *Report to Congress on Foreign Government Treatment of U.S. Commercial Banking Organizations* (Washington, D.C.: 1979).

Chapter 5

# The IMF and the World Bank: Measures to Improve the System

## Catherine Gwin

Amidst the current international debt turmoil, various measures have been proposed for dealing more effectively with the immediate crisis and with international financial problems over the longer term. For the most part, the proposals have either sidestepped the international financial institutions entirely or have called for a substantial increase in their control over credit decisions and in actual financial intermediation. The recommendations offered here chart a middle course: They seek to strengthen the role of the official institutions in the management of international finance while encouraging the further growth of open and competitive international capital markets.[1]

## Evolution of the Relationship Between Official and Private Lenders

From their start at Bretton Woods, the official institutions displayed a certain ambivalence toward private sources of credit. The Articles of Agreement of both the IMF and the World Bank make clear that the official institutions were intended to play primarily catalytic roles. Yet at the time of the Bretton Woods conference there was an undercurrent of distrust between governments and private lenders, stemming from events of the 1920s and 1930s. For example, as reported in a history of the formation of the Bretton Woods system:

[Henry] Morgenthau's dominant objective as Secretary of the Treasury was—in his own words—"to move the financial center of the world from London and Wall Street to the United States Treasury, and to create a new concept between nations in international finance." He wanted to erect new institutions which would be "instrumentalities of sovereign governments and not of private financial interests"—in short, 'to drive. . .the usurious money lenders from the temple of international finance.' Thus, the primary aim of the Treasury planners was not to restore a regime of private enterprise but to create a climate of world expansion consistent with the social and economic objectives of the New Deal.[2]

As a consequence, the interaction between public and private financial institutions has evolved slowly and uneasily.

In fact, until the 1970s neither the public nor the private sectors expected the private banking community to play a major role in promoting economic growth and development in the Third World. The presumption in the immediate postwar period was that most of the financial resources would come either from official sources or from foreign direct investment, which increased throughout the 1950s and 1960s. What was not anticipated was the slow start-up of both IMF and World Bank activities in developing countries. During the first five years of its lending (1947-52), the World Bank was not a major supplier of capital for either reconstruction or development.

When it became clear that the reconstruction task was too much for the fledgling international institution to handle, the Marshall Plan was set in place, and the World Bank then moved gradually into the business of development. In so doing, the Bank decided, for a number of reasons, to concentrate on making loans directly to developing countries rather than to use its guarantee authority to encourage developing-country borrowing from the private sector.[3] Therefore it increased its own borrowing from the private capital markets and expanded its direct lending to the developing world. The IMF, for its part, remained relatively inactive until the mid-1950s, and not until the 1970s did its lending activities become much involved with developing countries.

Thus through the mid-1960s neither the international financial institutions nor the commercial banks were major sources of capital for developing countries. By far the largest source of international financial flows to the developing world until then was bilateral official lending, which often took the form of tied loans or publicly insured or guaranteed supplier credits. It is perhaps worth remembering that these forms of financial flows themselves gave rise to debt-servicing difficulties. Also instructive are the recommendations of the major international report on the problems of development finance issued by the Pearson Commission in 1969:

> The procedures and principles for providing debt relief have often been inadequate. The primary objective of debt refinancing or consolidation has been to "bail out" the borrower by providing strictly short-run accommodation. The emphasis has usually been placed on speedy resumption of debt-service payments, rather than on re-establishing [a] financial framework for orderly growth. . . . *We recommend that debt relief operations avoid the need for repeated reschedulings and seek to reestablish a realistic basis for development finance.* The World Bank and the IMF. . . must of course participate in rescheduling discussions. . . . [We also] *recommend that, when it is necessary to set limits on new export credits, equal attention be given, where there is a sound development program, to the possible need for concessional external assistance.*[4]

The Pearson Commission also recommended that more official development assistance be channeled through multilateral agencies. A substantial relative increase in official development assistance from multilateral sources in fact did follow from the end of the 1960s through the 1970s. Yet over the same period official development assistance (ODA) as a whole contracted as a percentage of donor GNP (from 0.51 per cent in 1960 to 0.35 per cent in 1979). And what growth there was in ODA flows in absolute terms was dwarfed by the dramatic rise in commercial bank lending.

One reason for the rise in commercial bank lending was the sharp increase in Third World demand for credit from private banks that occurred just as the banks themselves were seeking to enter foreign markets. Although some developing countries began to borrow from the capital markets in the late 1960s to accelerate their growth and development, the reason developing-world demand for credit soared was the need to ride out the oil-induced recession of the mid-1970s. In response to the oil price shocks, the oil-importing countries of the Third World could have either sharply reduced their economic growth or run larger current-account deficits to be covered by borrowing abroad.[5] While their decision to seek financing for larger deficits was encouraged by industrial-country governments, the commercial banks quickly became the main source of developing-country financing.

Governments in both the industrial and the developing worlds and private lenders all had reasons for liking the recycling process that ensued. For the banks that took the lead in Third World lending, expected returns on foreign loans looked attractive and, the banks thought, the risks of sovereign lending were low. As more and more banks joined in the competitive scramble, they lowered profit margins on foreign loans; but at this stage of overseas expansion, the growth of assets was more important to the banks than return on assets. Furthermore, the introduction of floating-rate loans protected commercial lenders against the possibility that the cost of funds would rise more quickly than income from loans.[6]

For borrowers in the developing world, recycling offered more financing with less policy interference than when official lenders were the primary source. Not only was the volume of funds going to the Third World substantially higher, but credit was available more quickly. Agreements could be concluded in weeks or months, rather than in the two years typical for multilateral bank loans. More broadly, loans were made with few strings attached to either economic or foreign policies. And for a time, debt was a bargain. Bank competition led to declines in spreads and increases in the length of maturities, and in real terms, interest rates on loans were at or near zero through most of the 1970s and actually negative in the last years of the decade.

The governments of the industrial countries, for their part, were also glad to let the private markets provide deficit financing to developing countries. This relieved the public institutions of responsibility for managing the large-scale international financial dislocations resulting from the oil price hikes. Besides, continued developing-country growth somewhat eased the mid-1970s recession in the industrial countries by sustaining growth of exports to the developing world at a rate much higher than that of trade among industrial nations. Industrial-country governments did nothing, therefore, to moderate the pace of international borrowing. On the contrary, each time a problem arose, they sought to restore market confidence.[7]

## Sources of the Crisis

Despite the popularity of the recent refrain that governments should not "bail out the banks," the debt-servicing problems that erupted in the 1980s were not the result simply of too much borrowing and too much lending. Rather, the causes of the debt crisis were more complex and more deeply rooted. It is to those underlying causes that attention should turn in designing reforms for a more stable system in the future.

## Weakened International Defenses

As many informed observers have noted, the prolonged global recession of the early 1980s seriously undermined debt-servicing capabilities: The transition from world inflation to world recession and from negative to positive high real interest rates reduced export earnings, seriously weakened commodity prices, and sharply increased the cost of existing and new loans, thus creating a severe liquidity crisis for many borrowers. Moreover, the recession caught the world with weakened international defenses. Discussions begun in the late 1960s and early 1970s about making Special Drawing Rights (SDRs) the principal reserve asset of the system receded into the far-distant background as exchange rates were freer to float. IMF quotas (which determine the amount of resources available to the Fund and each member's relative access to those resources) were allowed to lag well behind the growth of international trade—declining from 16 per cent of world trade when the Fund was created in 1944 to 4 per cent at the start of the 1980s, and even further behind the rapid increase in capital movements. Although new IMF facilities were created in the 1970s to help countries adjust to the economic shocks of the period, the IMF still lacked both the resources and a clear mandate from member countries to foster smooth adjustments.

Indeed, after a loosening of conditions on IMF borrowing in mid-1979, the Fund tightened up its conditionality for access in mid-1981, leading one expert observer to ask whether "the developing countries should be expected to bear so much of the burden of curing world inflation; and whether the effort to defeat inflation by monetary restriction alone is well advised in light of the short-term costs."[8]

The Fund's sister institution, the World Bank, has concentrated over time on project rather than program lending. This focus not only has limited its ability to expand operations during a recession but also has given its lending a distinctly pro-cyclical character. Its Articles of Agreement mandate the World Bank to make project loans "except in special circumstances" (Article 3, Section 4, vii). The Bank has consistently followed a strict interpretation of this provision. As noted elsewhere:

> In fact, prior to 1980, non-project operations were undertaken only in response to a few cases of immediate and urgent need stemming from natural disasters or "man-made" ones (such as postwar reconstruction in Nigeria or Uganda); from serious declines in the terms of trade due to export price declines (such

as Zambia's past experience with copper or Colombia's with coffee); from import price increases (most obviously in the price of oil in 1973-74, and again in 1979); or from other acute needs such as India's need for help in financing imports of intermediate goods and spare parts for more fully utilizing its existing industrial capacity rather than for financing new projects.[9]

In 1980, the World Bank introduced a new form of non-project lending, the structural adjustment loan, in recognition that a deterioration in the balance of payments had become a major constraint on development. But the main feature of structural adjustment lending—its high degree of conditionality, focused on such considerations as the structure of incentives, public investment priorities, budgetary reform, and institution-building—has virtually precluded its applicability to emergency situations. Moreover, in an effort to minimize opposition to non-project lending, the SAL program has been limited to 10 per cent of total World Bank lending in any one year.

As world economic conditions deteriorated, the Bank introduced on a temporary basis an additional Special Action Program that, among other things, raised the limit on non-project lending and eased the requirement on the share of borrower-country coverage of project costs. But under the circumstances of prolonged recession and private credit contraction, the initiative was too little and too late to help countries avoid extremely steep cutbacks in their investment and growth strategies. One reason for the failure of the IMF and the Bank to respond more adequately to a deepening crisis was that the response needed fell into the gray area between the established roles of the two institutions—neither the Bank nor the Fund had a clear mandate to provide balance-of-payments financing in support of extended programs of economic adjustment. Therefore neither institution could take the steps required to prevent the burden of adjustment to the shocks of the 1970s from falling unduly on developing countries.

It could be argued that lenders and borrowers should manage their affairs as if depressions such as those of the early 1930s and early 1980s were always just around the corner. A more sensible approach, however, would seem to be to strengthen international non-inflationary defenses against serious slumps.

### The Legacy of Short-Term Loans and Variable Rates

A second underlying problem has been that the way debt evolved through the 1970s left borrower nations particularly vulnerable to the very economic pressures that erupted in the early 1980s. As noted by the World Bank in its 1983 *World Development Report*:

- Debt was increasingly composed of loans at variable rates, their share rising from less than 10 percent in 1970 to more than 40 percent by 1980. . . . [This eliminated] the interest rate risk for lenders [and thereby] made banks more willing to lend long-term during a period of rising inflation. Variable rates also promised to stabilize real interest rates on long-term debt, if interest rates changed in line with inflation. However, the tightening of monetary policy in major countries in recent years raised real as well as nominal rates.
- The practice of syndicating loans also helped to boost private financial flows to developing countries, by spreading the risks of such lending among many banks. With heightened uncertainty about economic prospects, however, banks have had to devote more resources to risk assessment, increasing their costs and discouraging some smaller banks from further lending. . . .
- Facing difficulty in obtaining long-term loans (official as well as private), countries looked increasingly to short-term borrowing or to running down their reserves. These expedients are customarily adopted to smooth out short-term fluctuations in earnings. Their use through the prolonged downturn of 1980-82 may have permitted a higher level of imports than would otherwise have been possible, but it has left many countries vulnerable to further shocks. By increasing their net short-term debt, countries also have become more exposed to rising interest rates and to sudden withdrawal of support by commercial banks.[10]

To these three observations should be added a fourth: The severe debt management difficulties now facing many developing countries might have been avoided if a broader mix of financial instruments had been used in the 1970s to finance new investments. In particular, increased reliance on commercial credit guaranteed by borrowing governments has led to a decoupling of debt-service costs from a country's ability to repay. Loans have entailed debt repayment obligations that hold irrespective of a borrower's export earnings, for example, and loans (as distinct from equity arrangements)—whether floating or fixed-rate—must be repaid without regard to the success or failure of particular projects, unexpected changes in terms of trade, or a country's overall macroeconomic situation. This creates little incentive for lenders to evaluate projects properly before the fact, or to contribute to their management once under way.

In contrast to pure debt instruments, equity-like financial instruments link the required repayments to outcomes. When these are favorable and the borrower is better off, creditors earn more, and *vice versa*. In addition to direct foreign investment, other arrangements with this type of feature include loans indexed to commodity prices or trade levels, constant payment factor floating-rate loans, non-recourse project loans, and production shares. Although it is not realistic to expect foreign direct investment and other, new forms of financing for developing countries to increase dramatically anytime soon, a change in the composition of capital flows to the Third World is desirable and the international financial institutions, in particular the World Bank, could help in this regard.

## Continuing Procedural Shortcomings

A third problem has been the shortcomings of procedures for handling debt-payment crises. Unfortunately, problems in this area persist despite useful innovations made in the recent rounds of stabilization and debt-rescheduling negotiations.

For more than a decade before the 1982-83 debt reschedulings, developing-country representatives as well as independent analysts had criticized the lack of coordination in debt-restructuring procedures and the tough terms that were meted out to the debtors, regardless of the cause of the debt problems they encountered or the repayment prospects they could anticipate.[11] Until the magnitude of the Mexican crisis became known, the shortcomings were largely ignored. Beginning then, however, a new approach for handling debt crises was used, involving simultaneous negotiations between debtor countries and international financial institutions, commercial creditors, and official creditors on the terms of multibillion-dollar "rescue packages." Typically, these have combined "bridge" financing from the Bank for International Settlements (BIS) and/or commercial banks, the rescheduling of commercial debt, provision of new bank loans, and additional financing from official creditors. Most notably, each element of a package has been made contingent upon all the others. For the first time, adjustment financing provided by the IMF thus has been made conditional not only upon policy changes in the debtor country, but also upon the extension of new credit by private banks without which the official financing measures would have been wholly inadequate.

In all cases, the most difficult element of the international rescue operations was the arrangement of new bank credits. The difficulty in this area arose mainly from the fact that so many different banks were involved, all with widely varying sorts of exposures. Moreover, the smaller regional banks were reluctant to participate in the reschedulings that they felt were drawing them far more deeply into international lending than they had anticipated when they made the original loans.

It was precisely to overcome this difficulty that the IMF undertook a newly activist role. As viewed from the private sector:

> The IMF exhorts banks to support those countries pursuing IMF adjustment policies, the banks exhort countries in difficulties to apply for IMF funds (and accept IMF conditionality), and the IMF carries out its most direct, prime function of exhorting countries to adopt and fulfill its recommended policies.[12]

In this way, the international financial community (governments, public institutions, and private lenders) has enabled debtor countries to keep debt payments current, but the system has not provided adequate means for helping countries with the broader task of serving their now-crippled economies. Nor has any international consensus emerged on how to deal with the underlying problems.

The strategy of the rescue operation has been for the debtor developing countries to adjust their economies to restore the current-account balance to equilibrium and for the banks to agree to reschedule principal due in 1983 and 1984 to relieve the debtors of amortization payments, at least for a time. Interest on the rescheduled loans is supposed to be paid when it is due, however—and, for a time in 1983, at higher rates—along with substantial fees to compensate the banks for rescheduling. New loans thus have been made to help debtors meet current interest payments, but with the net effect of increasing their indebtedness and financial outflows in the future. Moreover, the borrowing countries have had to slash imports and significantly reduce domestic standards of living, so that more of their export earnings will be available for interest payments and less new borrowing will be needed. This makes their external accounts look better but greatly weakens their internal economies, especially their manufacturing sectors.

One reason for the difficulties encountered by the debtor countries (in addition to the high real rates of interest) is that the creditors have insisted on rescheduling payments due for only one or two years at a time. This "short-leash" approach to rescheduling is said to be warranted by the enormous uncertainties in the world economy and by the difficulty of assessing the financial position of a debtor country over more than a year. But it is costly in terms of economic officials' time and makes it difficult for countries to deal with the structural problems that they must overcome to renew their growth. Indeed, the difficulties that stem from this approach have been widely acknowledged by participants in the reschedulings as well as by outside observers.[13]

In this immediate post-rescheduling phase, furthermore, before the market has regained full confidence, countries tend to face major difficulties in securing needed "recovery" financing. The limited availability of medium-term loans causes problems not only for the debt-burdened country—which, despite appropriate adjustment, will need financing to import capital and other goods essential to the resumption of economic growth—but also for that country's principal suppliers. In the present crisis, pressure being exerted on private banks by the IMF has succeeded in keeping some new credit flowing to the major debtor countries, but the amount of new lending often does not even cover the interest payments due.

Finally, it should be noted that one common characteristic of commercial debt restructurings in the early 1980s was a rapid expansion of increasingly short-term borrowing in a relatively short period of time, followed by a sharp decline, with net bank lending becoming negative just prior to a borrower's request for a restructuring. Had more information and better analysis been available at the time, the steep rise in short-term borrowing might have triggered "alarms" earlier on. And, as documented in a recent IMF study, timing is a significant factor in the effective handling of debt-servicing difficulties:

> Experience has shown that delays in initiating and concluding discussions frequently exacerbated the debt-servicing difficulties. Creditor confidence has tended to decline and creditors (including commercial banks) have slowed new lending and have withdrawn short-term financial credits, interbank deposits, and trade credits. This acted to jeopardize the quality of assets of lenders who did not or could not reduce their exposure. It also made the formulation of a viable balance of payments program more difficult.[14]

What is needed, however, is not just more information but also better analysis and judgment about individual countries and about aggregate borrowing and lending trends and capabilities. Various steps already have been taken by the IMF; by the newly established international banking institution, the Institute for International Finance; and by some debtor and creditor governments to provide more complete and timely data and analysis. These steps may bring about less of a "regionalization" of debt and less of a tendency for suppliers of very short-term credit (such as three-month trade credit) to cut off "normal" credit when countries encounter difficulties in servicing medium- and long-term debt. It seems unlikely that the measures taken so far are in themselves enough.

In addition, what has been described as a "governor on the market" seems to be needed to reduce the scope for wide swings in sentiment for and against a particular country or group of countries.[15] This does not mean that market judgment about the creditworthiness of an individual nation should be replaced with some official scheme of credit allocation. Instead, certain changes in the policies and procedures of the IMF and the World Bank should be undertaken to improve the monitoring of debt as well as to improve the processes of debt renegotiations and recovery—not by involving the two institutions more directly in the allocation or renegotiation of commercial debt, but by strengthening their roles in a number of activities supportive of open and competitive capital markets. Reforms that seem particularly desirable are discussed in the remainder of this chapter.

## Reforms for the Future

The financial crisis of the early 1980s and its underlying problems demonstrate all too dramatically the importance of strengthening the roles of the IMF and the World Bank. Consideration of reforms that should be undertaken is particularly appropriate now, in light of the renewed interest in and increased reliance on these institutions shown at the height of the debt crisis. For all but the poor and commercially non-creditworthy, the international institutions obviously are no substitute for the private capital markets, with their far vaster resources. The IMF and the Bank should, however, be better able to promote a more stable system of international finance conducive to sustainable, non-inflationary growth. To this end, specific reforms should be undertaken in the policies and procedures of the IMF and the World Bank to:

- Improve these institutions' capability to help countries absorb the international economic shocks and cycles that will from time to time disrupt national economies and threaten the stability of the international system;
- Strengthen each institution's catalytic role in the promotion of additional, more stable, non-official financing; and
- Expand their activities in ways that will help smooth the process of crisis management.

### Cushioning the Impact of Shocks and Cycles

Strengthening the shock-absorber and counter-cyclical roles of the Fund and the Bank requires, among other things, finding some way to expand their net lending substantially during periods of global recession. The purpose of this is not to shift the burden of financial costs from commercial banks to the general public, but to help minimize the risk that liquidity problems will lead to a financial collapse that might, in turn, spark widespread depression to the detriment of all. One way to do this would be to vary Fund conditionality counter-cyclically.[16] This reform is intended to avoid a repetition of the situation that occurred in 1981, when the Fund tightened conditionality in the face of severe world recession.

Although the decision to ease conditionality is simple and straightforward in concept, in practice it is likely to be a highly politicized matter. An alternative approach—expanding the IMF's Compensatory Financing Facility (CFF)—therefore might be more effective.[17] The existing CFF compensates countries for a shortfall in export earnings or a rise in cereal import costs. An enhanced CFF would provide a desirable "first line of defense against depressions" and give greater protection to the poorest countries, which regularly lack access to private credit and tend to have the fewest defenses of their own against international economic instabilities and shocks. Although an enhanced CFF would, in principle, benefit all member countries of the Fund that experienced a drop in export earnings, in practice it would most assist the poorer developing countries, which have the least access to commercial credit.

In building better defenses against serious shocks and slumps, it might also be desirable to introduce into the IMF a special interest-rate facility to provide relief for borrowers in situations like the present one, in which abrupt hikes in interest rates are caused by factors as much beyond their control as floods or droughts—for which the IMF has long compensated countries through the CFF when commodity export earnings plunge.[18] This seems a legitimate function for an intergovernmental organization, especially inasmuch as government policies can be a cause of interest-rate movements up or down. But the acceptability of the proposal would also seem to depend on governments undertaking a number of other reforms in the regulatory sphere and in procedures for managing debt-payment crises that would oblige private lenders to act in a responsible manner conducive to international economic stability and growth.

An increase in program (non-project) lending by the World Bank could also help countries to absorb economic shocks. Although project financing is useful in times of economic expansion, it has to be reduced in times of economic recession, when a borrower country cannot afford its own share of a project's cost. In contrast, program lending can serve a country both in times of economic growth to supplement foreign-exchange earnings for a robust investment program and in times of recession to help promote adjustment and sustain imports in the face of lower earnings. Moreover, a substantial increase in World Bank non-project lending would seem to correspond well with anticipated trends in future lending by the commercial banks—which have lost much of their enthusiasm for balance-of-payments financing and now seem inclined to concentrate more on project-linked financing.

Strengthening the counter-cyclical role of the international financial institutions should also include some means to help them foster more prudent growth of credit in expansionary periods. This is obviously more difficult to accomplish, since neither the Fund nor the Bank is a main source of financing for most countries in the world, and since neither has the authority to tighten the spigots of private credit.

In fact, striking an appropriate balance between credit restraint and stimulation is the issue at the center of current debates on how to strengthen supervisory and regulatory control of international bank lending. Central banks are today in the ambiguous position of pressuring commercial banks to increase exactly the country exposure that the authorities, in their supervisory roles, must criticize and may punish. In response to this situation, the Group of Thirty has recommended that central banks should regularly agree on a growth range for international lending that would be acceptable, while using their own instruments to achieve this.[19] Writing in his individual capacity, the Chairman of the Group of Thirty (and former IMF Managing Director) Johannes Witteveen has gone one step further and proposed an international insurance facility under the auspices of the IMF that would provide insurance on a conditional basis: to debtor countries following an agreed IMF course and to banks in those creditor countries that agreed to international reserve requirements.[20] Although this proposal would centralize credit-flow decisions beyond a point that nations are likely to find acceptable today, the Group of Thirty's recommendation does not go far enough in bringing a systemic perspective to bear on the assessment of overall credit needs.

No single change in existing regulatory or supervisory procedures can produce the desired results. Rather, a combination of steps—within commercial banks, by national regulatory authorities, and involving the international financial institutions—is probably needed to strengthen the decision-making processes for international lending. At the global level, it would seem desirable to institute the kind of central bank discussions proposed by the Group of Thirty but to bring these within the ambit of the IMF, involving the Managing Director in an advisory capacity as "the governor of the system." This arrangement would draw on the analytical capabilities of the IMF staff while leaving any supervisory and regulatory measures in the hands of national authorities acting independently. In turn, the IMF ought to be mandated to play a greater role in monitoring international financial flows, in maintaining a regular dialogue with borrowers and creditors alike regarding financing trends and the policies that affect them, and—in recognition of the links that exist between finance and trade—in cooperating more closely with the General Agreement on Tariffs and Trade (GATT).

Although such measures would not eliminate economic shocks or cycles, they would help cushion the disruptive impact of such events and, thereby, help reduce the likelihood of future financial crises.

## Catalyzing Non-Official Financing

Both the IMF and the World Bank should also take steps that would enhance their respective catalytic roles. For the most part, such steps could be undertaken without major budgetary costs to their member countries. In the mid-1970s, as commercial bank lending rose dramatically, the World Bank initiated the practice of co-financing projects with private lending as a way to tap international sources of private capital for development purposes. And in the early 1980s, the Bank introduced additional co-financing features, including arrangements whereby it could participate directly in syndicated loans, to make the practice more attractive. This initiative represents one way in which the Bank has sought to strengthen its catalytic role.[21] But the predominant view from the private sector and from those who have studied the possibilities of co-financing is that the effect is likely to be marginal in terms of additionality—partly because of the World Bank's unwillingness to take on cross-default obligations and partly because the commercial banks prefer to decide on their own to whom they will lend and for what purposes. The influence that the Bank and the Fund are able to exert on policies affecting the macro-economic context within which lending and investing decisions are made remains their main means of encouraging additional financial flows from other, far vaster sources of capital.

It has always been difficult, however, to get countries to come to the international financial institutions for conditional financing in good times—especially when private credit is cheap and readily accessible. Countries turn to the Bank and the Fund when they get into difficulty, but often not until their situations have so deteriorated that they have few options. To encourage nations to follow a different course, it would be desirable, as others have suggested, to alter the terms of reference of the IMF's Extended Fund Facility

(EFF) to make clear that its purpose is to aid countries to adjust to structural deficits, and that—since this is an inherently lengthy process—it will tend to be associated with a need for substantial financing.[22]

Raising the ceiling set on World Bank non-project lending—discussed earlier in the context of easing the impact of shocks—would likewise be a useful step in helping countries to create a policy environment conducive to sustainable growth and, in turn, attractive to private lenders. Moreover, in increasing their respective roles in the promotion of policy reforms to achieve orderly structural adjustments, the Fund and the Bank will need to further their recent efforts to work more closely together in negotiations of country adjustment programs and country policy dialogues.

As developing countries seek to find new, *non-bank* sources of development financing, the World Bank also could and should play a more active role in helping countries diversify the range of their development financing instruments. It could, for instance, begin to use creatively its long-standing guarantee authority as a way to advance innovative financing techniques. Many new techniques and instruments have been proposed, no single one of which, however, is likely to be appropriate for all developing countries. The World Bank could, it would seem, provide individual countries with technical assistance, where needed, to design a diversified financing strategy; play a role in matching borrowers with creditors; and provide a guarantee where that would help to "close" an innovative deal. Indeed, according to some market analysts, the World Bank could, in making use of its guarantee authority, count guarantees as only a fractional charge against the Bank's lending level without impairing its own standing in the credit markets, thus making guarantees an instrument for additional financing.

### Improving Debt-Crisis Management

Buttressing the counter-cyclical and catalyctic roles of the international financial institutions in these ways should help make the system less crisis-prone. Debt-servicing difficulties will nevertheless continue to arise from time to time. To minimize disruptiveness, two additional reforms—one involving the IMF and the other the World Bank—should be undertaken in an effort to improve crisis management to the benefit of borrower and creditor alike.

First, while the Fund has performed an important role as a crisis manager in the recent round of debt renegotiations and should be encouraged to do so again if need arises, it might take a somewhat different approach in the future, by "topping off" the commercial loans that are made as part of restructuring exercises: Instead of simply adding its lending to that of the commercial banks at the time of a debt renegotiation, the Fund might offer financing that would lengthen the maturity structure of a country's debt and thereby help to smooth out future repayment streams. Such action by the IMF should, moreover, be instituted as part of a broader, improved approach to debt renegotiations.

Although both bankers and borrowers have opposed the idea of a more "structured" approach toward the renegotiation of sovereign debt, perhaps some further innovation will seem more attractive after the turmoil of the present rounds of negotiations and renegotiations. At least there will be a large body of case histories that might help to move all parties toward some measure of agreement—if not a formal code—on the distribution of responsibilities in debt renegotiations, even though each of these will continue to be handled case by case. Such a code might link debtor-country negotiation of a program of adjustment with the IMF to creditor willingness to, at a minimum, maintain exposure levels through the restructuring period on terms no less favorable than in the initial loan agreement. Moreover, guidelines might be set for multiyear restructurings involving repayment schedules tied to some measure of a debtor's capacity to repay (for example, the amount of monthly debt service might be determined by a formula based on net export receipts and capital inflows). This idea has been endorsed by the Latin American debtor countries that signed the Cartegna Consensus of June 1984 as well as in assessments of recent debt renegotiations made by individuals closely involved in the process.[23]

Some understanding might also be reached on procedures for handling the repayment (and/or capitalization) of interest in a period of steeply rising rates. Moreover, the IMF might be expected to set "contingent conditions" in its own financing agreements that would provide for adaptation of performance criteria in adjustment agreements in light of changed circumstances (such as the rate of inflation).[24] Even if a formal code were not possible, informal acceptance of these sorts of "rules of the game" could contribute to more orderly debt reschedulings.

Second, there would seem to be an important role for the World Bank in the recovery phase after debt renegotiations. Building on its relations with and knowledge of a member country, the World Bank could, at the request of a debtor government, assess the country's medium- to long-term resource needs and then try to act to mobilize funds for a comprehensive "recovery program." The World Bank's activities, as proposed here, would not be the same as either the role that the IMF has played in putting together an "emergency rescue package" or the World Bank's own traditional role in organizing aid consortia: On the assumption that voluntary new lending will pick up again quickly once a country has launched an adjustment program, the IMF focuses on short- to medium-term steps, while the Bank acts more slowly, in the context of extensive analysis of a country's long-term development picture, and tends to involve only official creditors. What is missing is precisely the new, long-term investment financing in support of economic recovery that is most needed immediately after a rescheduling and before private investors have regained full confidence in the country's economy.

The World Bank's role in this process would not entail shouldering the major financing burden. It also would not eliminate the continuing need for political pressure and support from bilateral sources in a debt rescheduling exercise. Nor would it preclude a role for central banks in extending new credit after a rescheduling. But as a practical matter, the World Bank is in a good position to bring a government and its potential sources of new credit together once a rescheduling is completed and to help frame the medium- to long-term economic picture.

One component of this "recovery phase" role for the World Bank might, in fact, take the form of a proposed mechanism now under discussion in the International Finance Corporation (IFC), the private-sector affiliate of the World Bank. The IFC proposes establishing investment trusts for individual developing countries. Trust shares, denominated in dollars, could be issued to new investors as well as to interested commercial bank participants in exchange for some of their existing loans to private- and public-sector borrowers. The trust's manager (probably a New York investment bank) would then try to swap the loans for equity stakes in local enterprises. A big advantage of the scheme would lie in the eventual marketability of investment-trust shares, which, with IFC/World Bank backing, might be attractive to institutions such as pension funds. Moreover, the marketability of the investment-trust shares should mean that the commercial banks would be able to sell their shares at a smaller discount than they now concede when selling their loans directly. What is particularly attractive about the scheme is that it addresses both the developing countries' immediate financial problem of having attracted more foreign loans than they can cope with and their longer-term development financing problem of receiving less foreign equity capital than they need. Thus the proposed investment trusts could contribute to recovery as well as to long-term improvement in development financing, which includes reducing debtor-country dependence on commercial bank borrowing and replacing that form of credit with other sources of external finance.

## Information and Analysis

Finally, to complement all of these activities, the flow of information between countries and their creditor banks could and should be improved with the help of the international financial institutions.[25] This might not only help prevent the type of "regionalization" of a debt crisis recently experienced in Latin America but also help alert creditor governments and official financial institutions to impending troubles that might come to require (as the early 1980s demonstrated) emergency official actions to head off widespread international financial turmoil. In discussing this point, a recent American Express Bank paper made what would seem to be just the right assessment:

> There is little point in banks asking to be given access to confidential Fund-member government discussion papers. Such access would merely stop such confidential information being made available to the Fund, or unnecessarily hamper its already sensitive dialogue and consultation procedures with members. To take a private banking analogy, an investment banker to a corporation can hardly be expected to divulge corporate information to other banks in the market, except at the consent of the company itself—and certain discussions will always remain confidential.
> 
> But the Fund can encourage countries to publish more data (especially debt data). Countries rarely suffer from such publicity, and those who are able to efficiently publish debt information have generated thereby a good reputation for debt control and management.[26]

To this should be added the further recommendation, however, that the Fund provide more technical assistance to countries seeking to develop their national capabilities to collect, assess, and disseminate financial and other economic data. The staff of the World Bank has noted a close linkage between inadequate national provision of information and subsequent debt-servicing difficulties. The problem of overcoming inadequate debt reporting by countries is of course political as well as technical:

> Prompt and comprehensive information on the volume and tenor of new debt contracted by the public and private sectors can be obtained only where *national information-gathering*

*agencies* are given sufficient independence and authority to command the supply of information and to face their governments with the facts, welcome or otherwise. The political sensitivity of such a role is believed to have impeded fuller information flows from a number of debtor countries.[27]

The Fund has taken a cautious approach to technical assistance in this area in order to avoid having such aid perceived by client countries as unwelcome policy advice. Yet the need for wide-ranging technical assistance is great in a number of countries—and could be particularly beneficial for the Fund's poorer and less developed member countries. It therefore seems that a bolder effort on the part of the Fund, especially in the context of increased funding and a broad range of reforms, would be appropriate.

The reforms proposed here—for changes in the practices of both the IMF and World Bank—do not aim to enlarge the role of the official institutions at the expense of private and national decision-making authority. Their intent is to diminish the disruptiveness of intermittent economic shocks, minimize market inefficiencies, and reduce the trauma of debt renegotiations in ways that can, in sum, help make the international financial system less crisis-prone and more conducive to sustainable growth.

## Notes

[1] This paper draws heavily on *Beyond Debt Crisis Management: An International Institutional Response* (New York: Carnegie Endowment for International Peace, September 1984)—a report prepared by the author for the Carnegie Endowment's Study Group on international financial cooperation in the 1980s. The Study Group, which met several times during 1982-83, included international financial experts from the U.S. policy-making, business, and academic communities.

[2] Richard N. Gardner, *Sterling-Dollar Diplomacy in Current Perspective*, rev. edit. (New York: Columbia University Press, 1980), p. 76.

[3] Edward S. Mason and Robert E. Asher, *The World Bank Since Bretton Woods* (Washington, D.C.: The Brookings Institution, 1973), p. 107.

[4] *Partners in Development*, Report of the Commission on International Development (New York: Praeger, 1969), pp. 156-58.

[5] In 1970, the total current-account deficit of all oil-importing developing countries equaled $8.6 billion. By 1975, the deficit had risen to $37.1 billion. It then dropped the following year to $25.3 billion and remained close to that figure until after the second round of oil price hikes in 1979, when it jumped again to $43.7 billion. In 1980, the deficit rose to $73.3 billion, and in 1981 to $88.2 billion, before beginning to decline, in 1982, to $82.4 billion. World Bank, *World Development Report, 1982* (New York: Oxford University Press, 1982), p. 13.

[6] Floating-rate notes are typically medium- to long-term instruments that are repriced every six months in line with a reference interest rate.

[7] Karin Lissakers, "Faustian Finance," *Foreign Policy*, No. 51 (Summer 1983), pp. 162-63.

[8] John Williamson, *The Lending Policies of the International Monetary Fund*, Policy Analyses in International Economics, No. 1 (Washington, D.C.: Institute for International Economics, 1982), p. 51.

[9] Stanley Please, "The World Bank: Lending for Structural Adjustment," in Richard E. Feinberg and Valeriana Kallab, eds., *Adjustment Crisis in the Third World* (New Brunswick, N.J.: Transaction Books, for Overseas Development Council, 1984), p. 85.

[10] World Bank, *World Development Report, 1983* (New York: Oxford University Press, 1983), pp. 21-22.

[11] Chandra Hardy, *Rescheduling Developing Country Debts, 1956-80: Lessons and Recommendations*, Monograph No. 15 (Washington, D.C.: Overseas Development Council, 1981).

[12] American Express Bank, *The AMEX Bank Review*, Vol. 10, No. 8/9 (September 15, 1983), p. 4.

[13] For example, according to a survey conducted by the Group of Thirty, most bankers and bank supervisors interviewed agreed that "it is unlikely that the stretchings out of principal repayments recently negotiated or still in the course of negotiation will, of themselves, prove sufficient to restore the full debt-servicing capacity of many of the debtor countries. Even if the recovery in world output and trade now started is maintained, as hoped, a number of countries may still need to return to the bargaining table with their international bankers to renegotiate the terms of principal repayments falling due in 1984, those falling due in the year after and, even, perhaps in the year after that." See M. S. Mendelsohn, *Commercial Banks and the Restructuring of Cross-Border Debt* (New York: Group of Thirty, 1983), p. 7.

[14] E. Brau et al., *Recent Multilateral Debt Restructurings with Official and Bank Creditors*, Occasional Paper No. 25 (Washington, D.C.: International Monetary Fund, 1983), p. 12.

[15] Anthony M. Solomon, "Some General and Some Summit-Oriented Comments on International Cooperation," Remarks before the International Center for Monetary and Banking Studies, Geneva (April 8, 1983).

[16] Williamson, *Lending Policies*, op. cit., p. 51.

[17] The proposal is for a "reinvigorated" facility that would focus on expected real export earnings (rather than nominal magnitudes, as at present). It would cover all exports. And shortfalls from expectations would be fully and automatically covered (or if "full and automatic" coverage were deemed too permissive, available credits would nonetheless exceed present quota-linked ceilings). See Carlos Diaz-Alejandro, "International Financial and Goods Markets in 1982-83 and Beyond," mimeographed, March 1983.

[18] For mention of this kind of facility, see "Debtors' decision," *The Economist*, June 16, 1984, p. 11.

[19] Mendelsohn, *Commercial Banks*, op. cit., p. 11.

[20] H. Johannes Witteveen, "Developing a New International Monetary System," Per Jacobsson Lecture (September 15, 1983).

[21] See, for example, emphasis on co-financing in A. W. Clausen, "The World Bank and International Commercial Banks: Partners for Development," Remarks delivered to International Monetary Conference, Vancouver (May 25, 1982).

[22] Williamson, *Lending Policies*, op. cit., pp. 58-59; see also Tony Killick et al., "The IMF: Case for a Change in Emphasis," in Feinberg and Kallab, *Adjustment Crisis*, op. cit., pp. 59-81.

[23] Richard S. Weinert, "International Finance: Banks and Bankruptcy," *Foreign Policy*, No. 50 (Spring 1983), pp. 138-49; Christine Bogdanowicz-Bindert, "Debt: Beyond the Quick Fix," *Third World Quarterly*, Vol. 5, No. 4 (1983), pp. 828-38.

[24] Williamson, *Lending Policies*, op. cit., pp. 40-41.

[25] See Christine A. Bogdanowicz-Bindert and Paul M. Sacks, "The Role of Information: Closing the Barn Door?," Chapter 3 in this volume.

[26] American Express Bank *AMEX Bank Review*, op. cit., p. 10.

[27] Mendelsohn, *Commercial Banks*, op. cit., p. 11.

Chapter 6

# High Finance, High Politics

Benjamin J. Cohen

International banking in the Third World used to be regarded as a straightforward commercial business. Banks compared loan opportunities in domestic and foreign markets, toted up the costs and benefits of alternative lending strategies, and allocated their resources accordingly. Even with formal political-risk analysis thrown in, financial decisions were ostensibly divorced from any considerations of foreign policy. High finance, in principle at least, was kept quite separate from the high politics of international diplomacy.

That era is over. The global debt crisis has become a central political issue in relations between the United States and the Third World. Indeed, debt now heads the agenda of the North-South dialogue. More international negotiating time is devoted today to the painful process of debt rescheduling than to any other single issue of interest to developing nations. At one time, banks might have thought that they could handle the problem on their own. But since the Mexican crisis two years ago, it has been well understood that, for the largest Third World borrowers at least, there can be no simple commercial solutions: The issue has become politicized and contentious. Debt is increasingly significant in determining not just economic but also political relationships with the South.

What are the key foreign policy implications of this issue for the United States? In this analysis, the focus is on the risks and opportunities that have been created for U.S. diplomacy in developing nations. The risks of the debt crisis are evident: possible financial disruption, loss of export markets, a souring of political relations, instability or disorder in areas of vital strategic importance. Less obviously, the crisis may also create opportunities for the United States to win good will and influence in the South. Keeping both possibilities in mind, this chapter briefly examines how U.S. political relationships in the Third World have been affected on balance—not only bilaterally but also via multilateral institutions like the International Monetary Fund—and seeks to identify initiatives that either U.S. banks or the U.S. government might undertake to minimize potentially adverse developments and/or capitalize on positive ones.

U.S. foreign policy is understood here to encompass the full range of strategies and actions developed by the government's decision makers in U.S. relations with other nations. Foreign policy aims to achieve specific goals defined in terms of national interests as perceived by decision makers themselves. National interests may include economic objectives no less than political or security concerns. All, however, are pursued through international diplomacy—a process that is inherently political in nature. In that sense, foreign policy *is* politics. The key question is the *degree* of "politicization"—the extent to which specific issues, economic or otherwise, have moved beyond the merely routine and technical ("low politics") to become matters of vital national importance ("high politics"). When that happens, political relationships are affected whatever the nature of the issue. The argument here is that the United States has now reached that point in its relations with the Third World as a result of the global debt crisis. High finance has become high politics.

## New Policy Linkages: For Better or Worse?

U.S. commercial lending to Third World countries influences both the issues of salience for U.S. foreign policy and the nature and scope of options available to policy makers. Not only has the effectiveness of existing foreign policy instruments in many instances been altered. In addition, key policy "linkages" have been created, impelling connections between different instruments or issue areas that might not otherwise have been considered necessary, as well as offering opportunities for connections that might not otherwise have been thought possible. U.S. banks now operate as important independent actors on the world stage, having been intimately involved in all the major sovereign debt crises of recent years. Foreign policy decisions have become far more complex in that the banks' interpretation of their private interests in the marketplace does not necessarily coincide with the public interest as interpreted by policy makers in Washington.

For some observers there is no question that, from a foreign policy point of view, the impact of international banking has been negative. By their decisions affecting sovereign borrowers—should they lend or reschedule debt? for what countries? how much? when? at what cost? under what conditions, if any?—banks establish priorities with respect to capital-importing nations that are tantamount to foreign aid decisions. And since these decisions may depart quite substantially from the recognized goals and priorities of official foreign policy, they could in turn hamper significantly the effectiveness of existing policy instruments. The U.S. government could find it more difficult to support or reward its friends, or to thwart or punish its enemies. Generous new loans or debt assistance to countries with poor human-rights records, for instance, or to regimes that support international terrorism could easily undermine efforts by Washington to exercise influence through the withholding of public money. Governments deemed vital to U.S. security interests could be seriously destabilized if they were suddenly "redlined" by the financial community. Contends Representative Jim Leach of Iowa: "The large money center banks are the true foreign aid policy makers of the United States."[1]

There is some truth to this charge. Banks do assume a political role when they lend on any large scale to sovereign borrowers, changing the nature of the constraints and opportunities that now confront public officials in the international arena. What is not at all clear is that these changes are necessarily disadvantageous for foreign policy. It depends on the circumstances. Indeed, insofar as the flow of credit correlates positively rather than negatively with movements of the diplomatic barometer, bank decisions actually may enhance, not diminish, the effectiveness of existing foreign policy instruments. The Nixon administration's campaign against Salvador Allende after his election in 1970 was undoubtedly strengthened by the drying up of private credits in Chile. Government support of such strategic allies as the Republic of Korea and the Philippines is undoubtedly reinforced by a continued high level of bank lending there. Sometimes private and public interests converge, sometimes they do not.

In any event, the impact on political relationships in the Third World will depend a great deal on the policy linkages that are created as a result of bank decisions. Debt-service difficulties are a natural breeding ground for policy linkages. When key sovereign borrowers get into trouble, Washington may feel forced to respond, however reluctantly, with some sort of support—in effect, to alter existing trade-offs among policy objectives by underwriting the debts in some way. This may be because the borrowers are considered too crucial for U.S. interests to ignore. As the Senate Foreign Relations Committee staff has written, the United States "has important security interests in other debtor countries. . . .It can hardly afford to stand by and watch the economies of these countries collapse, or to have their governments undermined politically by financial difficulties."[2] Or Washington may respond because of concerns about possible repercussions on the health and stability of U.S. banks or the wider financial or economic system. Either way, debtors gain a new kind of leverage to extract concessions from the U.S. government that might not otherwise be obtainable. These concessions may be financial, trade, or even political.

Financial concessions are the most familiar. Back in 1979, for example, Turkey, at a point near bankruptcy, was able to exploit its strategic position within NATO to persuade the United States and other Western allies to come to its rescue with pledges of special assistance totaling nearly $1 billion. (Subsequent aid packages for similar amounts were pledged for 1980 and 1981 as well.) More recently, financial assistance has been arranged for several Latin American debtors when they had trouble meeting their obligations to foreign creditors.

There may also be trade concessions. Although less familiar, these are increasingly mooted in Washington today despite strong domestic protectionist pressures. Policy makers have been forced to acknowledge the obvious linkage between trade and finance: Import liberalization may be the only way for major borrowers to earn their way out of debt morass. In the words of Myer Rashish, President Reagan's first Under Secretary of State for Economic Affairs:

> We must face the interdependence of the financial and trading systems. External debt only makes sense if the borrower has a reasonable prospect for servicing the debt by exporting goods and services to the lenders. . . .Ultimately, we, the lenders, will be confronted with a decision—either to open our markets in order to provide outlets to the borrowers for their exports, thus generating revenues in the borrowing countries for debt repayment, or to yield to protectionist pressures and be forced to deal with resultant financial failures.[3]

Finally, even political concessions may seem necessary. In 1977 the Senate Foreign Relations Committee staff worried that:

> There appears to be a direct correlation between economic hardship and political repression in many countries. The Carter Administration may therefore have to choose between

pressing its international human rights effort, and supporting creditor demands for drastic austerity programs that can only be achieved at the expense of civil liberties in the countries that undertake them.[4]

In the 1980s this dilemma obviously continues to confront the Reagan administration, in Latin America and elsewhere. In the case of the Philippines, for example, Asia's second largest debtor to the banks, a choice has been made to maintain support for the martial-law "New Society" of Ferdinand Marcos on broad foreign policy grounds; the need to preserve the financial viability of an important strategic ally is perceived to justify strict domestic controls, including the continued stifling of political opposition, in the Philippines.

The costs of any of these concessions could be considerable. But so too could be the benefits—not just in the sense of directly reducing the risks of the debt crisis, but also indirectly, insofar as such efforts win additional good will or influence for the United States. The challenge for U.S. diplomacy is to manage such policy linkages in a way that minimizes potentially adverse developments while capitalizing on potentially positive ones. In part, this will depend on the nature of any concessions made. And in part, it will depend on the ability of policy makers to influence the parallel commercial decisions of banks.

If policy makers are able to alter bank behavior to conform more closely to their own objectives—in effect, to deploy the banks as part of the government's linkage strategies—the effectiveness of U.S. diplomacy may be enhanced. Such an approach admittedly is not without risks. Any attempt to inject foreign policy considerations into private-bank decision making (such as by urging bank lending to a friendly but non-creditworthy country) could conceivably endanger bank safety and soundness. The subject is controversial. Yet the risks do not seem unmanageable in principle, and if in practice they are successfully managed, the net benefits to U.S. diplomacy could be considerable. The calculus for policy makers is complex. In an environment not entirely of their own making, they must balance the private commercial interests of banks with the public interest in stable, political relations with the Third World.

## Coping with Crisis in Latin America

The complexity of the calculus has been amply demonstrated by events over the last two years in Latin America, where almost two thirds of all developing-country bank debt is concentrated. Fears of financial disruption, sparked by the Mexican crisis, initially led

Washington into unprecedented financial concessions, which in turn won the United States considerable good will and influence in the region. In the short run, the impact on political relationships was positive. But as the debt crisis has worn on, and particularly as Washington's efforts to revive private lending to Latin America have largely proved ineffective, relations have grown more strained; the good will of our Hemispheric neighbors has been eroded. Over time, should the trend persist, the diplomatic position of the United States in the region could be critically jeopardized.

The roots of the Latin American debt crisis go back at least to the late 1960s, when a number of governments in the region made a deliberate decision to finance accelerated domestic investment with borrowing from private and public institutions abroad. Superimposed on this was the first oil shock, which spurred further borrowing to pay for higher-priced oil imports—followed by a trend after 1976 toward negative real interest rates in global financial markets, which whetted appetites even further. By the time of the 1979 oil shock, many Latin American governments were seemingly addicted to foreign finance, despite a return to positive real interest rates, and debt was piling up at a dizzying pace. By mid-1982, the total debt of the region had swollen to nearly $300 billion, including $90 billion for Mexico, $75 billion for Brazil, $30 billion each for Argentina and Venezuela, and $15 billion for Chile. Two thirds of the total was owed to banks.

Not surprisingly, the banks were getting worried. Already, two years earlier, they had begun to shorten the maturities of new credits, hoping thereby to position themselves to get their money out quickly should something go wrong. That would have been a rational policy for any one creditor acting alone. But with all banks doing it together, the practice merely added to the risks of lending to the region by greatly increasing the aggregate amount of debt that repeatedly had to be rolled over. By mid-1982, the debt-service ratio (including amortization) of the five largest debtors had grown to 179 per cent in Argentina, 129 per cent in Mexico, 122 per cent in Brazil, 116 per cent in Chile, and 95 per cent in Venezuela. In these five countries, interest payments alone were expected to sweep away from 35 to 45 per cent of export revenues. A storm was brewing.

The first threatening clouds appeared in the spring of 1982, during the Falkland Islands (Malvinas) conflict, when Argentina began to fall behind in its debt service due to the British government's freeze of Argentinian assets in London. But the really rough weather did not set in until the summer, when political and economic uncertainties in Mexico sparked a major capital flight. In

June, the Mexicans were still able to raise $2.5 billion in the Eurocurrency market, albeit with considerable difficulty. By August, new private lending had ceased, the peso had to be devalued, and the government was forced to announce that it could no longer meet its scheduled repayments of principal on external public debt. Suddenly, one of the Third World's two largest debtors seemed on the edge of default. The tempest had broken.

The U.S. government rushed to the rescue (like the cavalry of old, only this time on behalf of the Mexicans), quickly providing more that $2.5 billion of emergency assistance—$700 million via the Federal Reserve's swap arrangement with the Bank of Mexico, $1 billion from the Commodity Credit Corporation, and an advance payment of $1 billion on oil purchases by the Department of Energy for the U.S. Strategic Petroleum Reserve. In addition, the Treasury Department's Exchange Stabilization Fund (ESF) and the Federal Reserve together contributed about half of a $1.85-billion "bridging" facility provided through the Bank for International Settlements (BIS). And Washington also backed a proposed $3.9-billion credit from the International Monetary Fund. By September 1982 the Mexican situation seemed, for the moment at least, in hand.

But the storm kept spreading. The Mexican crisis virtually stopped new private lending to Latin America as bank confidence sagged, and soon other debtors in the region were deep in trouble too. More rescue packages had to be organized. In the fall, some $1.23 billion was made available to Brazil by the ESF. And in December 1982 and January 1983, bridging loans for both Brazil and Argentina were arranged through the BIS, with substantial U.S. participation. In addition, banks were constantly exhorted to resume their lending to the region, despite already high exposure levels. Typical was a well-publicized speech by Federal Reserve Chairman Paul Volcker in November 1982, which placed great stress on easing the difficulties of major Latin borrowers. "In such cases," he said, "new credits should not be subject to supervisory criticism."[5] Translated, this meant that considerations of banking prudence would not be allowed to prevail over the objective of keeping key debtors afloat. Banks were reportedly even threatened with closer scrutiny of their books if they did *not* go along with fresh loans for countries like Mexico.

Unfortunately, such pressures so far have proved to be largely ineffective. Substantial new lending to the region has still not been resumed. In 1980 and 1981, total bank claims in Latin America rose by some $30 billion a year. In the eighteen months from June 1982 to December 1983, by contrast, they increased by no more than $9 billion. And this was actually less than the total of "involuntary" lending arranged in connection with parallel IMF credits (more on that later), meaning no new "voluntary" or "spontaneous" lending at all. As a result, over the last two years only one important borrower in the region (Colombia) has been able to maintain debt service without some interruption. All major borrowers have had to enter into protracted and difficult negotiations with private and public creditors, and all have had to initiate painful—as well as politically risky—domestic austerity measures. In the words of Pedro-Pablo Kuczynski: "Undoubtedly, the interruption of significant new lending by commercial banks has been the major stimulus for such measures."[6]

Effective or not, however, Washington has continued to press the banks for a more accommodating attitude. In the case of Argentina, for example, the *New York Times* reported in the fall of 1983, after the country's presidential election, that:

> The bankers. . .said that they were already coming under pressure from the United States. . .to aid the country's new democracy after nearly eight years of military rule. Many are resigned to making some concessions.
>
> "We don't want to look like the bad guys," one American banker said.[7]

More recently, officials have also been urging the banks to consider limiting the interest rates they charge on loans to hard-pressed debtors. In May 1984, Federal Reserve Chairman Volcker suggested in another well publicized speech that "one of the things certainly worth looking at is what arrangements could be made so that one particular important threat to their financial stability, the continued rise in interest rates, could be dealt with."[8] What he had in mind was some kind of a "cap" on interest payments, with any excess of market rates over the cap being added to loan principal ("capitalized"). A specific proposal along these lines—for a cap tied to real interest rates—was floated by the Federal Reserve Bank of New York at a meeting of central bankers in early May 1984.[9]

Moreover, to encourage the banks Washington has continued to put its own money where its mouth is. The U.S. contribution to the IMF quota increase, finally approved by Congress in the fall of 1983, was one example. Another was the decision of the Export-Import Bank in mid-1983 to extend new loan guarantees of up to $1.5 billion to Brazil and up to $500 million to Mexico, the largest such package ever proposed by the Bank. William Draper, the Bank's president, made no secret of official intentions to prompt further private lending to these and other Latin countries: "We expect the proposed financing will strengthen the Mexican and Brazilian recovery by acting as a catalyst for continuing support by the international financial community."[10] What was most unusual about the initiative was that, unlike most such proposals, these guarantees were not even tied to any specific projects. The U.S. government wanted to send a signal.

Why the government has taken such an active role in the crisis is not difficult to discern. On broad foreign policy grounds, Latin America has always been regarded as a region vital to U.S. national interests. From the moment Mexico's difficulties began, there was never any doubt among policy makers that the security of the United States, rather than just Mexico's, was at stake—that the United States, too, would be threatened by serious economic or political instability south of the border. Nor was there any doubt that the contagion of disorder could spread to other Latin American nations as well. We simply could not ignore the potential for chaos in our own backyard, which might be sparked by financial default.

More narrowly, policy makers were of course also worried about the direct risks to American banks, particularly the large money-center banks, whose loan exposure in Latin America was substantial. In Mexico alone, at the end of 1982 exposure in relation to capital exceeded 40 per cent in nine of the twelve largest U.S. banks. Taking Latin America's five biggest borrowers (Argentina, Brazil, Chile, Mexico, and Venezuela) together, the exposure of these same dozen banks ranged from a low of 82.5 per cent of capital (Security Pacific) to a high of 262.8 per cent (Manufacturers Hanover), with most banks falling in a range of 140-180 per cent.[11] The banking system was vulnerable.

Finally, there was also concern about U.S. trade interests in Latin America. By 1982, the region had surpassed all but Western Europe as a market for U.S. goods; Mexico alone was now the third largest customer of the United States. Once the Mexican crisis broke, commerce and real-estate markets throughout the American southwest were seriously damaged. U.S. government officials never tired of stressing how many exports, and hence jobs, would be lost if something were not done for troubled debtors. Washington's motives were neatly summarized by Paul Volcker:

> The effort to manage the international debt problem goes beyond vague and generalized concerns about political and economic stability of borrowing countries. . . .The effort encompasses also the protection of our own financial stability and the markets for what we produce best.[12]

Given these several motives it is hardly surprising, then, that the government played such an active role. It is also not suprising, given the reluctance of private banks to resume lending to the region, that Washington's concerns gained debtors leverage to extract official concessions of some sort. What is striking is how much good will and influence were initially generated for the United States as a result. U.S. officials reported a marked shift toward a more accommodating spirit on the part of Latin governments on various international issues. The United States was now in a position to say, when looking for cooperation, that "we were there when you needed us, now we need you." In Brazil, Washington's efforts to help out financially were reported to have given the United States "more leverage...than it has enjoyed in more than a decade."[13] Suddenly the Brazilians were willing to talk about problems that had been roiling relations with the United States for years—including, most importantly, nuclear policy and military cooperation. Likewise, in Mexico diplomats noted a toning down of Mexican criticisms of U.S. policy in Central America, and the Department of Energy was permitted to buy an extra 40 million barrels of oil, at attractive prices, for the U.S. Strategic Petroleum Reserve.[14] In the short run, Washington's investment in these countries' financial stability seemed to yield significant foreign policy dividends.

But only in the short run. As the debt crisis has persisted, Latin governments were bound to grow more impatient under the pressure of growing domestic resistance to prolonged austerity measures. Outbreaks of rioting and street demonstrations, as well as recent election results, suggest a lower tolerance for belt-tightening in the region. Increasingly, the question being asked is why the burden of adjustment should fall entirely on the shoulders of the debtors. What was first perceived as generosity on Washington's part is now being viewed more as miserliness and insensitivity. U.S. concessions, it is noted, have been strictly financial and, for the most part, strictly short-term. (All the loans included in the emergency packages for Argentina, Brazil, and Mexico, for example, had to be repaid within one year.) No trade concessions have been forthcoming at all—indeed, barriers have increased for key imports from Latin America, such as copper and steel—even as rising U.S. interest rates, universally blamed on the Reagan administration's huge budget deficits, have been adding to current debt-service burdens. Washington's emphasis on domestic "stabilization" translates, in the Latin mind, into nothing more than retarded development, increased unemployment, and declining living standards.

The risk is that this changing mood could eventually push Latin American governments toward alienation and confrontation with the United States. It could even lead toward their replacement by regimes far less friendly to U.S. economic or security interests. The straws are in the wind. In May 1984, the presidents of four of the region's largest debtors—Argentina, Brazil, Colombia, and

Mexico—met in Buenos Aires and issued a joint statement warning that they "cannot indefinitely" accept the "hazards" of current approaches to the debt crisis. Expressing concern over the effects of "successive interest rate increases, prospects of new hikes and the proliferation and intensity of protectionist measures," they cautioned that "their peoples' yearning for development, the progress of democracy in their region and the economic security of their continent are seriously jeopardized."[15] And these sentiments were emphasized as well in June 1984 at the broader meeting of eleven Latin debtors in Cartegena, Colombia, which concluded with a plea to the United States and other creditor countries—as well as to the banks—to accept a greater share of the burden of adjustment.

The continuing dramas of Argentina and Venezuela, both of which deliberately chose to go into arrears on their debts rather than submit to harsh austerity programs, attest to the decline of patience in the region. Other regional governments are also considering a reordering of their domestic and foreign priorities. As a recent report of the Americas Society pointed out: "In virtually every Latin American and Caribbean country, there are major pressures to turn inward, . . . to turn their backs on existing obligations, and to look to solutions which stress a higher degree of protection and greater state control."[16] Such a reversal of policy attitudes could severely threaten U.S. political relationships in the region.

## Can the IMF Serve U.S. Interests?

Direct bilateral relations with regions such as Latin America are not the only dimension of U.S. foreign policy affected by the debt issue. More indirect U.S. relations with the Third World, such as those through multilateral institutions like the IMF, have also been affected as debt has risen to the top of the diplomatic agenda. In good part because of the debt issue, U.S. policy toward the IMF has changed dramatically since the Reagan administration first came to office. Initially cool to any significant or rapid enlargement of Fund resources, the administration eventually became one of its strongest advocates. At least in part, this policy shift appears to have reflected an altered perception of how U.S. interests might be served by a strong IMF. Yet here too, as the crisis continues, Washington's short-run diplomatic gains have been significantly eroded.

During its first eighteen months, the Reagan administration actively sought to discourage any early increase of Fund quotas (which determine *inter alia* a member country's borrowing privileges). The Seventh General Review of Quotas, which raised quotas from approximately Special Drawing Rights (SDR) 40 billion to SDR 59.6 billion (the SDR is currently worth about $1.05), had just been completed in November 1980; another review was not formally required before 1983. Yet already it was becoming clear that the IMF's usable resources would soon be running low. Mostly as a result of the second oil shock and subsequent recession in the industrial world, the deficits of non-oil developing countries grew enormously: from $41 billion in 1978 to $89 billion in 1980 and $108 billion in 1981. Total borrowing from the Fund rose quickly, from under SDR 1 billion in 1978 (new loan commitments less repayments) to SDR 6.5 billion in 1980 and SDR 12 billion in 1981. As early as the spring of 1981, IMF Managing Director Jacques de Larosière was warning of an impending threat to the Fund's own liquidity position. Without a new quota increase, he insisted, the Fund itself would need to borrow as much as SDR 6-7 billion annually to meet all its prospective commitments.

Nonetheless, the Reagan administration remained adamant. To a large extent, its opposition was rooted in a critical view of IMF lending practices as they had developed during the Carter administration, particularly after the second oil shock. In early 1979, the Fund's Executive Board had issued a revised set of guidelines on conditionality that put new emphasis on the presumed "structural" nature of many members' balance-of-payments difficulties. The normal period for a Fund stand-by arrangement had traditionally been one year. Under the revised guidelines, stand-bys could be extended for up to three years if considered "necessary"—confirming a trend toward longer adjustment periods that had already been evident in programs financed through the Extended Fund Facility, first introduced in 1974, and the Supplementary Financing (Witteveen) Facility established in 1977. To the Reagan administration, this smacked of development lending in disguise, and was therefore totally inconsistent with the IMF's intended role as a limited revolving fund for strictly short-term balance-of-payments assistance. Administration spokesmen were especially critical of large low-conditionality loans, like the SDR 5 billion credit arranged for India in late 1981, and were not at all eager to facilitate more such arrangements in the future. At most, they said, the administration might be prepared to contemplate a quota increase of perhaps 25 per cent, and even for that they were in no particular hurry.

But then came the Mexican crisis—and with it, a dramatic shift in U.S. policy. Suddenly the administration *was* in a hurry. Not only did it pronounce itself in favor of an accelerated increase of quotas (and a more sizable one at that); now it wanted to go even further. At the Fund's 1982 annual meeting in September, Treasury Secretary Donald Regan suggested "establishment of an additional permanent borrowing arrangement, which would be available to the IMF on a contingency basis for use in extraordinary circumstances." And during the following months the Secretary pushed hard for formal consideration of such a proposal, surprising observers who had become accustomed to the administration's understood recalcitrance on the size and timing of any new IMF funding. Said one private banker: "Maybe there's a problem out there that we don't know about."[17]

With Washington no longer dragging its heels, it did not take long to work out the details. In February 1983, the IMF announced agreement on an increase of quotas from approximately SDR 61 billion to SDR 90 billion—a rise of 47.5 per cent. Furthermore, the Fund's General Arrangements to Borrow (GAB) were to be tripled, from approximately SDR 6.4 billion to SDR 17 billion, and for the first time were to be made available for financing loans to countries outside the Group of Ten—thus converting the GAB into precisely the sort of emergency fund that Secretary Regan had suggested in September. The U.S. share of these increases, which at prevailing exchange rates came to a total of some $8.5 billion ($5.8 billion for a quota increase and $2.7 billion for the GAB expansion), was finally approved by Congress in November 1983, after protracted lobbying by the administration. The enlargement of Fund resources was formally put into effect the following month.

A policy shift of this magnitude demands some explanation. At one level, the explanation was simple. There really was "a problem out there": the threat of a chain reaction of defaults in Latin America and elsewhere that could plunge the whole world into another Great Depression. The Reagan administration did not want to go down in history alongside the Hoover administration. It had to do something, and it seemed only natural to make use of the IMF, an instrumentality that was already in place.

At a deeper level, however, the explanation was more complex. Use of the IMF, some administration officials began to believe, might actually serve U.S. diplomatic interests more effectively than attempts to deal with debt problems on a direct bilateral basis. Any effort by Washington itself to impose unpopular policy conditions on troubled debtors would undoubtedly have fanned the flames of nationalism, if not revolution, in many countries. But what would be regarded as intolerable if demanded by a major foreign power might, it seemed, be rather more acceptable if called for by an impartial international agency with no ostensible interests other than the maintenance of international monetary stability. In short, the Fund might help to contain a potentially explosive situation. As the nation with the largest share of votes in the Fund (just under 20 per cent), and as the source of the world's pre-eminent international currency, the United States still enjoys unparalleled influence over IMF decision making. Through its ability to shape attitudes at the Fund, therefore, Washington could hope to exercise more leverage over debtors indirectly than seemed feasible directly, and at lower political cost.

On the issue of policy conditions, the Fund had begun to tighten its standards even before the Mexican crisis, owing in good part to the Reagan administration's active disapproval of earlier IMF lending practices. By the summer of 1982 its institutional attitude had already shifted back toward more rigorous enforcement of domestic austerity measures. Thus once the crisis exploded, Fund officials needed no persuasion to take on the role, in effect, of the "cop on the beat"—setting policy conditions for new or renewed credits and ensuring strict compliance with their terms. Following the Mexican crisis, nearly three dozen countries fell into arrears on their foreign loans; over the next year nearly two dozen of them had to negotiate debt relief of some sort with private and/or official creditors. In all these negotiations, and in others still pending, the Fund has become a central arbiter of access to, as well as the terms of, new external financing. Creditors now typically require that a debtor country first conclude a stand-by arrangement with the IMF subject to strict conditionality as a precondition to their own financial assistance. Many reschedulings also demand continued compliance with Fund performance criteria; on occasion, disbursements of new loans have even been timed to coincide with drawings scheduled under Fund stabilization programs. Clearly, the IMF spells financial relief—and, as such, exercises considerable leverage over the policies of troubled debtors.

Equally clearly, the Fund's leverage is resented. Throughout the Third World, the slogan is: "The IMF is a dirty word." The hand of the United States behind the IMF is increasingly evident to many. In this respect, too, Washington's gains were essentially short-run. Initially, U.S. interests were served by letting the Fund get out in front. But as the crisis has persisted, the veil has worn thin; more and more often criticism is focused on the perceived power behind the throne. Hence the growing dissatisfaction with what is viewed as Washington's miserliness and insensitivity. Intermediation by the Fund is no longer enough to protect U.S. relations with the Third World from strain.

The story is similar in the IMF's relationship with the banks. Initially, it seemed, U.S. interests might also be served by the Fund's ability to apply effective pressure to banks. As already mentioned, Washington's own exhortations to U.S. banks to resume lending in Latin America or elsewhere have largely fallen on deaf ears. Not so, however, with the Fund—which in several key instances successfully demanded specific commercial commitments as a precondition for its own financial assistance. In connection with its $3.9 billion arrangement for Mexico, for instance, which took some four months to negotiate, the Fund refused to go ahead until each of the country's 1,400 creditor banks first agreed to extend additional credit amounting to 7 per cent of their existing loan exposure (totaling some $5 billion in new bank money for Mexico). Likewise, before approving a loan of $5.5 billion for Brazil in February 1983, the Fund laid down a number of requirements for the banks: restoration of interbank credit lines to $7.5 billion; new loans of $4.4 billion; rollover for eight years of $4 billion in principal due in 1983; and maintenance of short-term trade credits at $8.8 billion. Similar conditions were attached to agreements with other countries as well, most notably to those with Argentina and Yugoslavia. The IMF's message to the banks was clear. In the words of Jacques de Larosière: "Banks will have to continue to increase their exposures. . .if widespread debt financing problems are to be avoided."[18]

Not that the banks were all that eager to cooperate—not at first, at least. Many simply wanted to get their money out as quickly as possible. De Larosière had to "knock heads together," as one official phrased it.[19] But eventually the banks themselves came to recognize the crucial importance of such "involuntary" lending in critical cases. Said one prominent U.S. banker: "It was clear that somebody had to step in and play a leadership role."[20] Said another: "The IMF sensed a vacuum and properly stepped into it."[21] Could anyone imagine the U.S. government taking such interventionist initiatives? In the first place, Washington has no jurisdiction over the banks of other countries (which account for well over half of total loan exposure). And second, even American banks would have been highly reluctant to take such direction straight from government officials. U.S. banks have traditionally placed great store in their arms-length relationship with the authorities, and they insist vehemently on their right, as competitors in the marketplace, to make their own commercial decisions. In this respect, too, diplomacy seemed to be served by letting the Fund get out in front.

Once again, however, the gain has been essentially short-term. What the banks tolerated in certain critical cases will not become acceptable, they themselves say, as a general rule. Certainly they may again be prepared, should similar emergencies arise in the future, to surrender temporarily some of their traditional operating autonomy. But they will not accept a permanent role for the IMF in the management of private international credit flows, and they increasingly reassert their right to do as they see fit. Washington cannot rely opportunistically on Fund intermediation with the banks either.

## Seeing the Debt Crisis For What It Is

The global debt crisis has confronted Washington with a critical foreign policy dilemma. In political terms, the key issue is whether the governments of debtor countries will be able to work through the crisis without being pushed toward alienation from or confrontation with the United States. The crux of the problem lies in the austerity measures so far relied upon, which have bought time for debtors mainly at the cost of retarded development and lowered living standards. If social or political disorder, which could jeopardize U.S. economic or security interests, is to be avoided, growth must be resumed. At the same time, to honor their external obligations, countries will certainly need more help from abroad—from the banks and from the creditor nations, led by the United States. The burden of adjustment can no longer fall exclusively on the debtors. Therein lies the challenge for U.S. diplomacy.

Action is needed at three levels:

1. *Additional financial or non-financial concessions will be necessary to keep U.S. political relationships in the Third World from going sour.* Washington must acknowledge that there is a real risk of erosion in its political relations in the Third World if the growing perception of U.S. miserliness and insensitivity on the debt issue is not reversed. Nothing would help more than an altered fiscal and monetary policy mix in the United States to bring down interest rates.[22] Beyond that, Washington could make a significant contribution by substantially increasing direct credit and guarantee programs designed to sustain essential imports of raw materials, spare parts, and capital goods into debtor countries. In particular, the guarantee and insurance activities of the Export-Import Bank should be further expanded, building on the precedent of the package proposed for Brazil and Mexico last year. The government should also actively support increased funding for the multilateral development institutions, including both the World Bank group and the regional development banks. The direct budgetary cost of such initiatives would not be great. And the benefits, in political terms, could be considerable.

But even such concessions will not suffice if debtor countries are unable to earn the foreign exchange they need to pay their own way. Markets must be open to their exports: Trade concessions are needed as well. It does Brazil or Mexico little good to receive new loan guarantees from the Export-Import Bank if they are then hit with new duties on their steel exports. Chile and Peru will have even greater difficulty servicing their debts if barriers are raised to protect U.S. copper producers. It is time for Washington to ensure that what is given with one hand is not taken away with the other. This means avoiding any new restrictions on imports from Third World debtors. It also means considering reduction of existing restrictions on a non-reciprocal and, if need be, unilateral basis. In its Caribbean Basin Initiative, the Reagan administration has already demonstrated the possibility of legislating one-way import liberalization despite strong domestic protectionist pressures. Much political capital could be gained by extending that initiative to encompass all of our Hemispheric neighbors, and perhaps even other strategically important debtors such as the Philippines or the Republic of Korea.

2. *The government needs to make a determined effort to persuade banks to take more explicit account of the foreign policy implications of their commercial decisions.* A more accommodating attitude toward debtor countries on the part of the banks is essential if political relationships with the Third World are to remain stable. By their rescue of Continental Illinois, the U.S. regulatory authorities demonstrated their determination to avoid failure of any large American money-center bank, no matter how substandard its loan portfolio may be. Most observers interpret this as, in effect, underwriting the U.S. banking system's substantial investment in Third World debt—which, in turn, removes any excuse banks may have thought they had to keep the debtors on a "short leash." The banks must accept some of the costs of resolving the present crisis, as Karin Lissakers argues in Chapter 2. They should be encouraged to consolidate and reschedule debt on a multiyear basis, stretching out loan maturities as much as possible in order to reduce and smooth annual amortization payments, as well as to lower their interest charges to the extent feasible. In particular, consideration should be given to an interest-rate cap that would permit "capitalization" of a portion of interest payments currently due. More broadly, greater coordination is called for between the agencies responsible for prudential supervision of banks—the Federal Reserve, the Comptroller of the Currency, the Federal Deposit Insurance Corporation—and those responsible for foreign policy in the more traditional sense of ensuring adequate financial resources for countries of political or strategic importance to the United States.

3. *To avoid further aggravation of an already explosive situation, the United States must maintain its support for a strong IMF.* Adequate resources are essential if the Fund is to continue exercis-

ing any kind of effective role at all in relation to debtors and banks in the current crisis. Despite last year's enlargement of quotas and the GAB, more resources may soon be needed. Arrangements to borrow from member countries should be expanded to the extent possible. More important, the United States should take the lead in supporting borrowing by the Fund from private markets, if necessary, to supplement its liquidity position. And in the absence of an interest-rate cap, speedy consideration should also be given to creation of a new interest-rate stabilization facility within the Fund along the lines suggested in Chapter 5 by Catherine Gwin, to help protect debtors against unexpected interest-rate increases. The cost of such a facility could be shared by both governments and banks.

In short, the United States must confront the debt issue for what it is: as much a *political* problem as an economic one. The practical difficulties of implementing the appropriate policy actions should not be underestimated, but neither should the dangers to U.S. diplomatic interests if they are not. The risks are great, but so, too, are the opportunities to win good will and influence in the developing world. High finance can no longer be kept separate from high politics. Today, they are one and the same.

## Notes

[1] As quoted in *New York Times*, November 11, 1982, p. D3.
[2] U.S. Senate Committee on Foreign Relations, *International Debt, the Banks, and U.S. Foreign Policy*, A Staff Report (Washington: 1977), p. 7.
[3] Myer Rashish, "Bank Lending Overseas Has Become Intertwined with Politics," *American Banker*, January 15, 1982, p. 6.
[4] U.S. Senate Committee on Foreign Relations, *International Debt*, op. cit., p. 7.
[5] Paul A. Volcker, "Sustainable Recovery: Setting the Stage," Remarks before the New England Council, Boston, November 16, 1982, mimeographed, p. 17.
[6] Pedro-Pablo Kuczynski, "Latin American Debt: Act Two," *Foreign Affairs*, Vol. 62, No. 1 (1983), p. 24.
[7] *New York Times*, November 5, 1983, p. 46.
[8] *New York Times*, May 13, 1984, p. 1.
[9] *New York Times*, May 11, 1984, p. D2.
[10] As quoted in *New York Times*, August 18, 1983, p. 1.
[11] William R. Cline, *International Debt and the Stability of the World Economy* (Washington, D.C.: Institute for International Economics, 1983), p. 34.
[12] As quoted in *New York Times*, June 4, 1983, p. 29.
[13] *New York Times*, November 15, 1982, p. D1.
[14] *Miami Herald*, August 30, 1982.
[15] *New York Times*, May 21, 1984, p. D1.
[16] Americas Society, *Report of the Western Hemisphere Commission on Public Policy Implications of Foreign Debt* (New York: 1984), pp. 19-20.
[17] As quoted in *New York Times*, December 12, 1982, Section 3, p. 1.
[18] As quoted in *New York Times*, January 9, 1983, Section 3, p. 10.
[19] Ibid.
[20] Ibid.
[21] Ibid.
[22] See Colin I. Bradford, Jr., "The NICs: Confronting U.S. 'Autonomy'," in Richard E. Feinberg and Valeriana Kallab, eds., *Adjustment Crisis in the Third World* (New Brunswick, N.J.: Transaction Books, for Overseas Development Council, 1984), pp. 119-38.

# About the Overseas Development Council and the Contributors

The Overseas Development Council is an independent, non-profit organization established in 1969 to increase American understanding of the economic and social problems confronting the developing countries and to promote awareness of the importance of these countries to the United States in an increasingly interdependent international system.

In pursuit of these goals, ODC functions as a center for political analysis, a forum for the exchange of ideas, and a resource for public education. Current projects fall within four broad areas of policy concern: trade and industrial policy, international financial issues, development strategies and development cooperation, and political and strategic aspects of U.S. economic relations with the Third World.

ODC's program is funded by foundations, corporations, and private individuals; its policies are determined by a governing Board and Council. In the selection and coverage of issues addressed by the current ODC program, including the new U.S.-Third World Policy Perspectives series, the ODC staff and Board also benefit from the advice of members of the ODC Program Advisory Committee.

John W. Sewell is president of the Overseas Development Council.

## The Editors

*Uncertain Future: Commercial Banks and the Third World* is the second volume in the Overseas Development Council's new series, U.S.-Third World Policy Perspectives. The editors of the series, Richard E. Feinberg and Valeriana Kallab, are both with the Council.

**Richard E. Feinberg** has been vice president of the Overseas Development Council since 1983. After coming to the Council in 1981 as a visiting fellow, he became an ODC senior fellow and director of the foreign policy program. From 1977 to 1979, Feinberg was Latin American specialist on the policy planning staff of the U.S. Department of State, prior to which he served as an international economist in the U.S. Treasury Department and with the House Banking Committee. He is currently also adjunct professor of international finance at the Georgetown University School of Foreign Service. Feinberg is the author of numerous books as well as journal and newspaper articles on U.S. foreign policy, Latin American politics, and international economics. His most recent book is *The Intemperate Zone: The Third World Challenge to U.S. Foreign Policy* (1983).

**Valeriana Kallab** is the Council's director of publications and senior editor. Before joining ODC in 1972 to head its publications program, she was a research editor and writer on international economic issues with the Carnegie Endowment for International Peace in New York. She was co-editor (with John P. Lewis) of *U.S. Foreign Policy and the Third World: Agenda 1983* and (with Guy F. Erb) of *Beyond Dependency: The Third World Speaks Out* (1975). She is a member of the U.S. National Commission for UNESCO.

# Contributing Authors

**Lawrence J. Brainard** is senior vice president of Bankers Trust Company, where he directs international economic and political analyses, is responsible for the organization of the bank's country risk assessment system, and serves as chairman of the country risk committee. Mr. Brainard has published widely on economic issues relating to Europe, both Eastern and Western, on international capital markets, and on developing countries. Since 1975, he has served as advisor on East-West commercial relations to the Atlantic Council, the Dartmouth Conference, the Office of Technology Assessment of the U.S. Congress, and the National Security Council. He is a member of economic committees established by creditor banks to evaluate economic development associated with debt reschedulings in Poland, Costa Rica, Yugoslavia, and Nigeria.

**Karin Lissakers** is currently writing a book about international banking to be published by Random House. From 1981 to 1983, she was a senior associate at the Carnegie Endowment for International Peace, writing about international banking and foreign policy. From 1978 to 1980, she served as deputy director of the policy planning staff of the U.S. Department of State and before that as staff director of the Senate Foreign Relations subcommittee on foreign economic policy. Ms. Lissakers wrote one of the earliest comprehensive studies of the Eurocurrency market and petrodollar recycling (1977), which warned of many of the problems that have now culminated in the debt crisis. Her articles on international banking have appeared in *Foreign Policy*, *The New York Times*, *The Washington Post*, and other publications.

**Christine A. Bogdanowicz-Bindert** is a senior vice president in the International Banking Division of Shearson Lehman/American Express. Since joining Lehman Brothers four years ago, her main responsibility has been to advise sovereign governments on a wide range of economic and financial issues and more particularly on negotiations with commercial banks. She has been involved in debt reschedulings in both Latin America and Africa. Prior to joining Lehman Brothers, she worked as an economist at the International Monetary Fund, where she helped governments develop stabilization programs and provided technical assistance on foreign exchange management. Before joining the IMF, Ms. Bindert worked for a commercial bank in Germany. She has published numerous articles on economic and financial issues, banking, sovereign debt rescheduling, stabilization programs, and African economies. Currently she is also teaching a course in international banking at the Graduate School of Business Administration at Fordham University.

**Paul M. Sacks** is managing partner of Multinational Strategies, Inc. (MNS), and heads the firm's growing consulting activities for financial institutions. Prior to joining MNS, Dr. Sacks worked at the Chase Manhattan Bank, where he helped develop the bank's political risk analysis system and served as Chase World Information Corporation's regional analyst for Western Europe. He is a specialist in international financial issues and Western European politics, with extensive overseas research experience in the United Kingdom, Ireland, France, and Nigeria.

**George J. Clark** is an executive vice president of Citibank, N.A., where he supervises corporate officers worldwide and is responsible for, among other things, the establishment of country risk/exposure lending limits. Mr. Clark joined Citibank in 1964 as an assistant vice president handling government and central bank relationships in the Western Caribbean and South America and was elected a senior vice president in 1969. He assumed responsibilities for the bank's operations in Canada, the Caribbean, Central and South America in 1973 and was placed in charge of operations in Asia and Africa in 1976. He assumed his present position in July 1981. Prior to joining Citibank, Mr. Clark was chief of the Caribbean Division of the International Monetary Fund. Before joining the IMF in 1956, he was deputy director of the Foreign Trade Administration of the Greek government's Economics Ministry in Athens.

**Catherine Gwin** is currently a consultant to both the Ford Foundation and the Asia Society. From 1981-83, she was senior associate of the Carnegie Endowment for International Peace, where she directed a Study Group on international financial cooperation and the management of developing country debt. From 1980-81, she was North-South issues coordinator to the United States International Development Cooperation Agency. From 1976-78, she was on the staff of the 1980s Project of the Council on Foreign Relations; she became director of the project in May of 1978 and held that post until December 1979. In addition, she taught at the School of International Affairs of Columbia University in the fall of 1978 and the spring of 1979. Dr. Gwin has published widely in the field of development economics. She currently serves on the Board of Oxfam America.

**Benjamin J. Cohen** is currently William L. Clayton Professor of International Economic Affairs and director of the William L. Clayton Center for International Economic Affairs at the Fletcher School of Law and Diplomacy at Tufts University. Prior to this position, he was assistant professor in the department of economics at Princeton University (1964-71) and an economist in the research department of the Federal Reserve Board of New York (1961-64). Dr. Cohen's work on international monetary problems and U.S. foreign economic policy includes six books—most recently *Banks and the Balance of Payments*—as well as numerous monographs and articles. Dr. Cohen has also contributed to many Congressional hearings. He is currently working on a book on international banking and U.S. foreign policy. Dr. Cohen has won a wide variety of honors—most recently the William H. Shepardson Fellowship of the Council on Foreign Relations.

# Overseas Development Council

## Board of Directors*

**Chairman: Robert S. McNamara**
**Vice Chairmen: Thornton F. Bradshaw**
             **J. Wayne Fredericks**

Marjorie C. Benton
William H. Bolin
Thomas L. Farmer**
Roger Fisher
Orville L. Freeman
John J. Gilligan
Edward K. Hamilton
Frederick Heldring
Susan Herter
Ruth J. Hinerfeld
Joan Holmes
Robert D. Hormats
Jerome Jacobson

William J. Lawless
C. Payne Lucas
Paul F. McCleary
Lawrence C. McQuade
Alfred F. Miossi
Merlin Nelson
Joseph S. Nye
John Petty
Jane Cahill Pfeiffer
John W. Sewell**
Daniel F. Sharp
Barry Zorthian

## Council

Robert O. Anderson
Robert E. Asher
William Attwood
Marguerite Ross Barnett
Douglas J. Bennet
Edward G. Biester, Jr.
Jonathan B. Bingham
Eugene R. Black
Robert R. Bowie
Harrison Brown
Lester R. Brown
Ronald B. Brown
John C. Bullitt
Goler T. Butcher
Frank C. Carlucci
Lisle C. Carter, Jr.
Kathryn D. Christopherson
George J. Clark
Harlan Cleveland
Frank M. Coffin
Owen Cooper
John C. Culver
Ralph P. Davidson

Richard H. Demuth
Charles S. Dennison
William T. Dentzer, Jr.
John Diebold
Albert Fishlow
Luther H. Foster
Arvonne Fraser
Stephen J. Friedman
Richard N. Gardner
Peter Goldmark
Katharine Graham
James P. Grant
Arnold C. Harberger
Theodore M. Hesburgh, C.S.C.
Philip Johnston
Vernon E. Jordan
Nicholas deB. Katzenbach
Philip H. Klutznick
J. Burke Knapp
Peter F. Krogh
Geraldine Kunstadter
Walter J. Levy
George N. Lindsay

\* *Board Members are also members of the Council.*
\*\* *Ex Officio.*

William McSweeny
Harald B. Malmgren
Edwin M. Martin
John Mellor
Robert R. Nathan
Rev. Randolph Nugent
Daniel S. Parker
James A. Perkins
James Phelan
Samuel D. Proctor
Charles W. Robinson
William D. Rogers
J. Robert Schaetzel

David H. Shepard
Eugene Skolnikoff
Davidson Sommers
Joan E. Spero
Stephen Stamas
C.M. van Vlierden
Alan N. Weeden
Clifton R. Wharton, Jr.
Thomas H. Wyman
Clayton Yeutter
Andrew Young
George Zeidenstein

## ODC Program Advisory Committee

**Chairman:**
**John P. Lewis**

Shahid Javed Burki
Albert Fishlow
James Galbraith
Jeffrey Garten
Denis Goulet
Davidson R. Gwatkin
Edward K. Hamilton
G.K. Helleiner
Albert O. Hirschman
Robert D. Hormats
Michael M. Horowitz
Gary Hufbauer
Peter B. Kenen

John Mellor
Theodore H. Moran
Joseph S. Nye
Kenneth A. Oye
Dwight H. Perkins
Gustav Ranis
Ronald K. Shelp
Robert Solomon
Joan E. Spero
Lance Taylor
Norman Uphoff
Nadia Youssef

Overseas Development Council
1717 Massachusetts Ave., N.W.
Washington, D.C. 20036
Tel. (202) 234-8701

A *New Series from the Overseas Development Council*

# U.S.-THIRD WORLD POLICY PERSPECTIVES

Titles already available or scheduled for joint publication by Transaction Books and the Overseas Development Council in 1984-85:

## ADJUSTMENT CRISIS IN THE THIRD WORLD
*Richard E. Feinberg and Valeriana Kallab, editors*

Just how the debt and adjustment crisis of Third World countries is handled, by them and by international agencies and banks, can make a big difference in the pace and quality of *global* recovery and development progress—upon which U.S. prosperity also depends. Stagnating international trade, sharp swings in the prices of key commodities, worsened terms of trade, high interest rates, and reduced access to commercial bank credits have slowed and even reversed growth and development in many Third World countries. Together, these trends make "adjustment"—both short-term financial stabilization and longer-range changes in the structure and content of production—the central problem confronting developing countries in the mid-1980s. Individual chapters in this volume analyze the longer-term outlook for managing Third World debt; the need for readjusting the policies of the IMF; the World Bank's structural adjustment lending program; and the adjustment experiences of the newly industrializing countries (NICs), Mexico, several Central American and Caribbean nations, and Brazil.

**Contributors:** Albert Fishlow, Tony Killick, Graham Bird, Jennifer Sharpley, Mary Sutton, Joan M. Nelson, Colin I. Bradford, Jr., Riordan Roett, Lance Taylor, and DeLisle Worrell.

*Richard E. Feinberg* is vice president of the Overseas Development Council. He previously served as the Latin American specialist on the policy planning staff of the U.S. Department of State, and as an international economist in the Treasury Department and with the House Banking Committee. His most recent book is *The Intemperate Zone: The Third World Challenge to U.S. Policy* (1983).

*Valeriana Kallab* is the Overseas Development Council's director of publications and senior editor. Before joining ODC in 1972, she was a research editor and writer on international economic issues with the Carnegie Endowment for International Peace in New York.

200 pp.                             ISBN: 0-87855-988-4 (paper) **$12.95**
No. 1, May 1984                ISBN: 0-88738-040-9 (cloth) **$19.95**

# U.S. FOREIGN POLICY AND THE THIRD WORLD: AGENDA 1985

*John W. Sewell and contributors*

The U.S. administration that takes office in 1985 will face a set of major challenges in putting U.S.-Third World relations on a positive track. The Overseas Development Council's 1985 *Agenda*—the tenth such U.S. policy assessment produced by the Council—will analyze recent U.S. policy performance and policy options in the areas of trade and industrial policy, international finance, development strategies, and political and strategic aspects of U.S. economic relations with the Third World. Extensive statistical annexes on U.S.-Third World economic transactions and indicators of economic and social development will again be provided.

 *John W. Sewell* has been president of the Overseas Development Council since January 1980. From 1977 to 1979, he was the Council's executive vice president, directing ODC's research and public education programs. His many articles and other publications on international development issues include "Can the North Prosper Without Growth and Progress in the South?" in the ODC's *Agenda 1979*, and *The Ties That Bind: U.S. Interests in Third World Development* (1982).

**160 pp.**           ISBN: 0-87855-990-6 (paper) **$12.95**
**No. 3, January 1985**      ISBN: 0-88738-042-5 (cloth) **$19.95**

---

# U.S. TRADE POLICY AND DEVELOPING COUNTRIES

*Ernest H. Preeg and contributors*

North-South trade relations are deeply troubled. U.S. exports to developing countries declined by $18.2 billion for 1980-83, at the cost of some 1.1 million jobs in the U.S. export sector. Many developing countries face financial crises that can only be resolved over the longer run through resumed expansion of trade. In this volume, distinguished practitioners and academics identify specific policy objectives for the United States on issues that will be prominent in the proposed new round of GATT negotiations: adjustment of U.S. firms and workers to imports from developing countries, including sensitive sectors such as textiles and steel; transition or "graduation" of the newly industrialized countries of East Asia and Latin America to a more reciprocal basis of access to markets; special benefits for the poorest or least developed countries; and preferential trading arrangements.

 *Ernest H. Preeg*, a career foreign service officer and currently visiting fellow at the Overseas Development Council, has had long experience in trade policy and North-South economic relations. He was a member of the U.S. delegation to the GATT Kennedy Round of negotiations and later wrote a history and analysis of those negotiations, *Traders and Diplomats* (The Brookings Institution, 1969). Prior to serving as American ambassador to Haiti (1981-82), he was deputy chief of Mission in Lima, Peru (1977-80), and deputy secretary of state for International Finance and Development (1976-77).

**192 pp.**           ISBN: 0-87855-987-6 (paper) **$12.95**
**No. 4, March 1985**       ISBN: 0-88378-043-3 (cloth) **$19.95**

# DEVELOPMENT STRATEGIES: A NEW SYNTHESIS

*John P. Lewis and contributors*

Contrary to the widespread popular view that few development efforts have worked, many Third World national development ventures in fact have been comparatively successful when measured against historical precedents. But growth rates have slowed, and the international economic environment is now much less favorable to growth and development progress than in the 1960s and even the 1970s. What has been learned from past development promotion experiences? And what approaches hold promise for the harsher economic circumstances of the 1980s and 1990s?

In this volume, prominent analysts of the development process—including experts (some from the Third World) with experience in both policy design and policy implementation—consider how to promote development effectively in the future. New syntheses of policy are proposed that seek to reconcile the goals of growth, equity, and adjustment; to strike fresh balances between agricultural and industrial promotion and between capital and other inputs; to reassess the strength and breadth of the case for outward-oriented strategies; and to reflect the interplay of democracy and development.

*John P. Lewis* is professor of economics and international affairs at Princeton University's Woodrow Wilson School of Public and International Affairs. He is simultaneously senior advisor to the Overseas Development Council and chairman of its Program Advisory Committee. From 1979 to 1981, Mr. Lewis was Chairman of the OECD's Development Assistance Committee. He has served as a member of the U.N. Committee for Development Planning, of which he was also rapporteur from 1972 to 1978. For many years, he has alternated between academia and government posts (as Member of the Council of Economic Advisors, 1963-64, and Director of the U.S. AID Mission to India, 1964-69), with collateral periods of association with The Brookings Institution and The Ford Foundation. His recent writings have focused on South Asian development and North-South economic relations.

**160 pp.**
**No. 5, May 1985**

ISBN: 0-87855-991-4 (paper) **$12.95**
ISBN: 0-88738-044-1 (cloth) **$19.95**